Nature Guide to
EAST ANGLIA
& Lincolnshire

ROS EVANS

Contents

Cover photographs:
Top: Bearded Tit, Oxlip, Red Squirrel
Centre: Avocet, Sea Lavender, Swallowtail
Bottom: Sunset and reeds

Title page photograph *(page 1)*:
The Ouse Washes

Edited by Karen Goaman

Series Editor: Karen Goaman

Designed by Anne Sharples

The editor wishes to thank Felicity Mansfield, who edited "Places to Visit", and Ros Evans and Mary Fane for picture research.

The author and publishers wish to thank Nicolette de Sausmarez for work on "Places to Visit", F. J. Bingley, J. Longhurst, R. Markham, C. Ransom and S. Thompson for additional help; also the following organizations for their help:

Cambridgeshire and Isle of Ely Trust for Nature Conservation, East Anglia Tourist Office, Essex Naturalists' Trust, Forestry Commission, Lincolnshire and South Humberside Trust for Nature Conservation, National Trust, Nature Conservancy Council, Norfolk Naturalists' Trust, Royal Society for the Protection of Birds, Suffolk Trust for Nature Conservation, Wildfowl Trust.

Most of the illustrations in the section on pages 33–96, Common Species of the Countryside and Seashore, have been previously published in the Usborne Spotter's Guides series.

First published in 1981 by
Usborne Publishing Limited
20 Garrick Street, London WC2

© 1981 by Usborne Publishing Limited

Printed and bound in Great Britain by
Fakenham Press Limited, Fakenham, Norfolk

Introduction

East Anglia's swamps, eroding and flooding coastline, and plains of mobile sands ensured for centuries that the region remained largely unspoilt by man. Even today it is relatively free of large-scale industrial and urban expansion.

So in East Anglia a naturalist's paradise still exists in the miles of wild and lonely coastline, with its wide horizons and immense unobscured sky. The vast expanses of mud teem with life and echo with the cries of wading birds. Extensive coastal marshlands are decked in summer with pink and mauve flowers. Between October and March the coast, while attracting few holidaymakers, attracts thousands of birds including migrants.

There are few other places in Britain where one can find nationally rare plants growing in profusion as they do in East Anglia in the Oxlip woods and the Fritillary meadows; or where one can be lured by the "churring" call of the Nightjar across sparsely-wooded heathland late at night; or where one can stand surrounded by acres of rustling reeds and listen to the "booming" call of the Bittern in the dusk.

This watery wetland world in East Anglia is protected from human disturbance by an impenetrable thicket of willows, alders and buckthorn.

How to Use this Book

The first section of this book, pages 4-32, illustrated with colour photographs and paintings, describes the habitats that are characteristic of East Anglia and the animals and plants special to the region. There is a colour map on pages 8-9 showing the areas in which the habitats mainly occur. Many habitats are closely linked to the geology and climatic conditions of the region: these features are described on pages 4-7.

The middle section of the book, pages 33-96, contains illustrations of over 350 species of animals and plants commonly found in East Anglia and over much of Britain. Further details on how to use this section are found on page 33.

The third section of the book, "Places to Visit", found on pages 97-117, consists of a gazetteer containing descriptions of over 180 places of interest. Each county of East Anglia has a separate list and a map showing the location of the sites. The places described include specific habitats, nature reserves, nature trails, birdwatching points, and also zoos, wildlife parks, country parks, gardens, and museums. Further details on this section are found on page 97.

Birds and flowers to look out for in the various habitats of East Anglia are listed on pages 118-121. Other information such as useful addresses, good reference books, and a full index are found at the end of the book. Use the index to find out whether a species is illustrated – page numbers referring to illustrations appear in bold.

When visiting the countryside, care should be taken to respect the habitats and the wildlife living there. Flowers should not be picked, nesting birds and mammals with young should not be disturbed, and the Country Code, set out on page 122, should always be followed. Nature conservation in East Anglia is also discussed on page 122.

Geology and Climate

East Anglia's areas of low relief and vast expanses of flatness, typified by the Fens and the coastal marshlands, are more extensive than in any other region of Britain. The whole region cannot however be described sweepingly as flat, since it consists of gently rolling countryside, dissected by numerous streams and rivers. In Lincolnshire, the limestone "cliff" and the Wolds form undulations which can almost be described as "uplands" by contrast with the neighbouring land.

The underlying geological features (the solid geology) are shown on the map opposite. The effects of the solid geology are however masked by superficial deposits (see page 6), which lie over most of the underlying rocks.

Both the solid geology and the superficial deposits greatly influenced the development of the habitats which characterize East Anglia. This can be seen clearly on the map (pages 8–9).

▼ Watery scene at sunrise: mud and saltmarsh at Gibraltar Point in Lincolnshire. Many miles of the region's coastline consist of wide, flat marshland, protected by spits, bars and sea walls.

Solid Geology

The map shows two important strata: the limestone "cliff" of west Lincolnshire, and the chalk which sweeps up from north-west Essex, across the Wash and up to its highest point in the Lincolnshire Wolds.

Both strata tilt in a generally eastward direction, sloping gently downwards deep below the North Sea, and present their eroded scarp slopes along their western edges. Between the limestone and the chalk, and in the east resting on the chalk, are beds of clay (including London Clay) and sand (crag sands and Greensand).

All these strata began as deposits on the floors of ancient seas. Chalk and limestone consist of the fossil remains of marine organisms. Chemically they are therefore very similar, the predominant feature being calcium carbonate which makes the overlying soils very alkaline, or sweet. Limestone is older and harder than the soft chalk, and weathers to give a very different landscape.

The crag sands too are very rich in shelly fossils and are therefore more alkaline than the pure acid (quartz) sand like the Greensands.

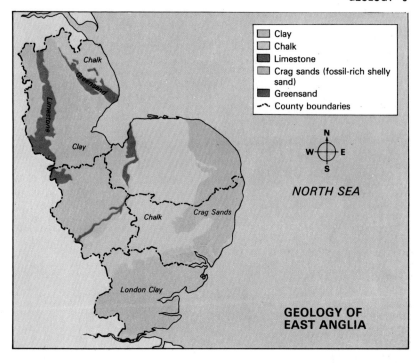

Clay
Chalk
Limestone
Crag sands (fossil-rich shelly sand)
Greensand
County boundaries

NORTH SEA

GEOLOGY OF EAST ANGLIA

▼ The Lincolnshire Wolds: scarp slope where the red chalk is exposed at Red Hill (a reserve).

Superficial deposits

During the Ice Age most of the region was covered with ice. Towards the end of the period, when the ice retreated, it left behind deposits – "glacial drift" – over most of the underlying rocks. The varying drift material can be seen on the map on pages 8–9.

The thickness of this glacial drift varies considerably, to the extent that in places it is non-existent. Its character also varies: commonly it consists of stony clays (boulder clay) with abundant chalk fragments (beige on the map), but there are also areas of sand and gravel (pink on the map). This sand and gravel was outwash material from melting glaciers or ancient river deposits.

The other significant deposits are of more recent origin and consist of peat and alluvium, laid down in shallow water (blue on the map). These occur mainly in the very low-lying districts such as river valleys, along the coast, and especially in the Fenland basin, where there are inland areas that are below sea level.

Effects of the Geology on the Habitats

The superficial deposits – that is the glacial drift and the peat and alluvium – mask the effect of the underlying rock. For instance, chalk and limestone grasslands (see page 24) which characterize chalk and limestone bedrock, are not nearly as extensive as would be expected if the solid geology was not covered by drift.

On the moist fertile boulder clays (of the drift), dense forest developed, whereas the drier sandier areas became covered by only sparse woodland. In both cases the trees were eventually cleared by man. The clay areas became herb-rich grassland while the sandy lands became heaths, both with their characteristic assemblage of wildlife. But now much of East Anglia's grassland and heathland has been converted to arable land.

The natural habitats occurring on the more recently deposited peats and alluvium include the coastal marshes, and the Fens and Broads of inland wetlands. Large portions of these unique habitats have also disappeared under the plough.

▼ Filby Broad (*left*) and Wicken Fen (*right*). The Fens and the Broads are both wetland habitats situated on peat and alluvial deposits that have accumulated since the Ice Ages.

These wetlands once predominated over a considerable portion of the region, human activity helping maintain a balance ideal for wetland wildlife (see page 13). In the seventeenth century however, large areas were drained to provide agricultural land.

Climate

East Anglia boasts the lowest rainfall and the highest summer temperatures in Britain. It also experiences some of the lowest winter temperatures. Its climate, although strictly oceanic (see below) is therefore more similar to a continental type of climate than that of any other region of Britain. The generally low-lying profile of East Anglia means that there is little variation in climatic conditions throughout the region.

Like the rest of Britain, East Anglia falls within the oceanic climate belt which is characterized by warm, moist conditions with comparatively few frosts. This climatic regime is induced by the prevailing south-westerly winds, which blow across thousands of miles of the Atlantic, becoming progressively heavier with moisture all the way. On reaching land, that is the British Isles, this moisture is shed, but by the time the winds reach East Anglia, much of this moisture has already been lost. This accounts for the comparatively low rainfall, which is at its lowest in the Breckland (see page 27), where the annual rainfall averages approximately 570 mm.

In winter, the coldest winds come from the north-east, and there is very little water – only the narrow North Sea – between eastern England and Scandinavia to ameliorate the winds during their journey from the arctic wastes. East Anglia can experience even lower winter temperatures than comparable altitudes in Scotland, for the North Sea is narrower off the coast of East Anglia than it is off Scotland.

Effect of the Climate on the Habitats

The variation in climatic conditions within the region is not sufficiently great to induce major changes in plant and animal communities (as occurs for example at different altitudes in mountainous regions of Britain). The variation however has a slight effect. The low rainfall in the Breckland prohibits the growth of certain otherwise common species like Red Campion and Bugle. Frost-tolerant plants such as the Breck catchflies thrive in the combined effects of the "continental" climate of the Breckland and its geology.

▼ Wangford Warren, a nature reserve in Breckland, where the effects of East Anglia's continental type of climate are most strongly felt.

In the Breck, the unique combination of climate, geology and past land use (see page 27) resulted in a habitat of wild, sparsely-vegetated country of sandy soils, the land continuously changing as sand-blows covered fresh areas.

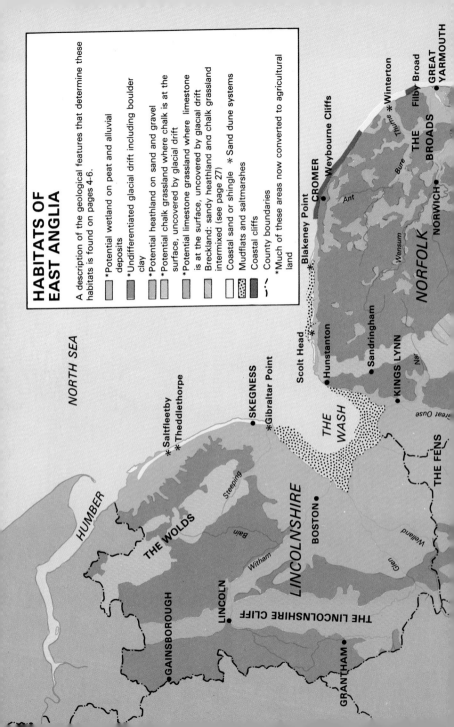

HABITATS OF EAST ANGLIA

A description of the geological features that determine these habitats is found on pages 4-6.

- *Potential wetland on peat and alluvial deposits
- *Undifferentiated glacial drift including boulder clay
- *Potential heathland on sand and gravel
- *Potential chalk grassland where chalk is at the surface, uncovered by glacial drift
- *Potential limestone grassland where limestone is at the surface, uncovered by glacial drift
- Breckland: sandy heathland and chalk grassland intermixed (see page 27)
- Coastal sand or shingle * Sand dune systems
- Mudflats and saltmarshes
- Coastal cliffs
- -- County boundaries
- *Much of these areas now converted to agricultural land

NORTH SEA

HUMBER

* Saltfleetby
* Theddlethorpe

SKEGNESS
*Gibraltar Point

THE WOLDS

Steeping
Bain
Witham

THE WASH

Scolt Head
*

Blakeney Point
*
CROMER
Weybourne Cliffs

Hunstanton

Sandringham

KINGS LYNN
Nar

Ant
Bure
Thurne * Winterton
Filby Broad
GREAT YARMOUTH

THE BROADS

NORWICH

NORFOLK

Wensum

LINCOLN

GAINSBOROUGH

THE LINCOLNSHIRE CLIFF

BOSTON

LINCOLNSHIRE

Welland
Glen

Great Ouse

THE FENS

GRANTHAM

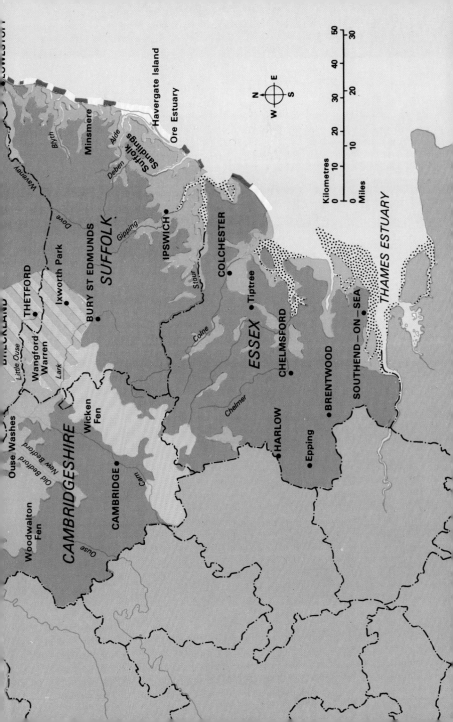

Wetlands

East Anglia, though the driest region in Britain, is nevertheless famous for its large areas of soggy and flooded land, notably the Fens and the Broads. These and the other wetlands – the many rivers, reservoirs and flood meadows, and the Breckland meres – are rich in wildlife.

Suffolk and Norfolk have the most extensive reed beds in Britain, providing important habitats for several rare birds. These include the Marsh Harrier, a bird of prey whose breeding ground in Britain is confined to East Anglia, the elusive Bittern, whose booming call in early summer signifies its presence, and the Bearded Tit or Reedling. Many waders find shelter in the wetlands, including the spectacular Ruff, and the Snipe, whose drumming in March is another sound associated with wetlands. Ducks occur, often in large numbers, and thousands of Wigeon and Bewick's Swans can be seen during the winter on the Ouse Washes. Otters are now confined to a few river valleys.

▲ Bewick's Swan: this species winters in a few areas of Britain, notably the Ouse Washes.

▲ The elusive Water Rail, usually seen retreating into dense reeds. Its long toes enable it to paddle across wet mud without sinking.

▼ Woodwalton Fen, a nature reserve. Only in the quieter fens and waterways can the rich variety of wetland wildlife thrive.

▲ Kingfishers, common in Britain but also shy, are sometimes seen fishing East Anglian rivers.

▲ The Snipe nests on marshes. Its courtship flight is accompanied by a drumming sound.

▲ Bearded Tit (male). Dependent on large reed beds for feeding and breeding, it is hence more common in East Anglia than in other regions.

▲ The natural habitat of the Harvest Mouse, now associated with cornfields, was probably once the more widespread wetland reed beds.

▼ An East Anglian reed bed, with a Bittern, seen in its hunched-up pose, and a Marsh Harrier on its nest. Both species nest in extensive reed beds.

Common Reed

Swallow

Bittern

Marsh Harrier

▲ Pochard (drake). A diving duck, it feeds in deep water on submerged plants. It breeds commonly in East Anglia, nesting in marginal vegetation.

▲ Shoveler (drake). A dabbling duck, it uses its spectacular bill with comb-like edges to sieve foodstuff from shallow water.

▲ The Great Crested Grebe builds its nest on undisturbed open water or under cover of reeds.

▲ Dragonflies (the Brown Hawker is shown) and Damselflies are seen patrolling still waters.

▲ The Swallowtail (*left*) and Large Copper (*centre*) were once widespread in the East Anglian wetlands. The Swallowtail is now confined to the Broads, and the Large Copper to one reserve. The Brimstone (*right*) lays its eggs on Buckthorn leaves – often the dominant bush of the carr.

▼ Though now rare, the Otter is potentially found wherever dense cover occurs near open water.

▼ Coypus, after escaping from fur farms, caused damage to waterways and are now controlled.

The **Norfolk Broads**, famous for boating and fishing, are also of great interest to the naturalist. They were first thought to be naturally formed, but it is now known that they are ancient peat diggings which flooded many hundreds of years ago when the level of the sea rose.

The name **Fenland** is still used to describe a considerable portion of East Anglia, although since the area was drained in the seventeenth century, there are in fact very few fens left. A fen, like a bog, is a wetland site where the substrate is peat as opposed to an essentially inorganic soil. Fens differ from bogs in that the pervading water is alkaline, or sweet, and therefore richer in nutrients, whereas in a bog it is acid, or sour, and nutrient-poor. Because of this, fens are able to support a wider and largely different range of plants. Although typical of East Anglia, fens are not restricted to this region, but are found wherever the above conditions prevail. Bogs are more characteristic of the north and west of Britain.

The Fenland is now a vast expanse of low-lying, rich agricultural land, interrupted by the occasional "island" of slightly higher ground. Before the seventeenth century, these were real islands in an extensive reed bed, giving way to open water in some areas and scrub (or carr) in others. The Fen people fed on fish and wildfowl; they cut osiers for their buildings, reed and sedge for thatch, and peat for fuel. With the regularity of these harvests, the land remained wet instead of being overgrown by carr and drying out as succession naturally took place (see below).

Attempts to drain the land, which was potentially some of the most desirable agricultural land in the country, started seriously in the seventeenth century but were not entirely successful until the invention of steam-driven pumps. Some areas were fortunately left undrained to take excess flood water in the winter. Some of this unreclaimed land was, and still is, used as summer grazing pasture – notably the Ouse Washes, which have become havens for wildfowl (and birdwatchers) during the winter. The floodlands which were not utilized in any other way gradually became overgrown by carr. Today

▼ *Succession*: this photo shows how wetland areas gradually become overgrown and dry out – a perfectly natural change called succession.
Open water: every autumn dead vegetation accumulates on the bottom and, since decomposition in this airless environment is minimal, peat forms and the water becomes shallower.
Open fen/reed bed: the fringe of reeds spreads into areas where the water was previously too deep for them to grow.
Carr: ultimately shrubs and trees start to invade the reed bed, drying out the land still further. This scrub is known as carr.

▲ The Broads: yachts alongside a load of sedge.

▼ A winter floodland in the Ouse Washes.

some of these have become nature reserves. In these reserves the aim is to recreate the diversity of habitat which resulted through the use of the land by the Fen people – clearing the carr, digging peat, and cutting reed and sedge.

The variety and beauty of the wetland plants can be seen in the open water, amongst the reeds and sedges, along river banks and marshland dykes.

Yellow is the colour displayed earlier in the year, with Marsh Marigolds, and then later with Yellow Flag, Great Yellowcress, the Spearworts, Yellow Water-lily and the floating Bladderwort. In the summer the water's edge may be festooned with shades of pink and purple, with Great Willowherb, Hemp Agrimony and Purple Loosestrife. The pale pink Water Violet is less widespread and is one of the plants found particularly in East Anglia. Many species of the Umbellifer (Cow Parsley) family belong to wetland, including Milk Parsley – food plant for the caterpillars of the Swallowtail butterfly. The British Swallowtail is a butterfly of fenland, which,

though once found in various parts of East Anglia, is now restricted to the Norfolk Broads.

Lowland wetlands are vastly richer in variety and abundance of wildlife than are the wetlands of upland Britain. This is because they tend to be located on more fertile land and are subject to milder climates. Many are also shallower and more sheltered. So a greater variety of plants thrive there, providing in turn a wealth of niches for animal life.

East Anglia's wetlands are now considered to be of great international importance for many species of wildlife. Unfortunately, wetlands are now the most threatened habitat not just in Britain but throughout the world. Too often they are drained to make way for agricultural land – and East Anglia's wetlands yield very fertile soil. In heavily populated areas, wetlands that escape drainage become attractive recreation areas; the Broads are an example. The effects of pollution and recreation produce extremely taxing problems not only for those concerned with wildlife, but also for neighbouring farmers.

▲ Reeds are still cut and bundled largely by hand, since heavy modern machinery would sink in the sodden peat of the reed beds.

▼ Reeds, still in demand for thatching; thousands of bundles are required for one cottage.

▼ Peat cutting was once a thriving industry in the fens. Once cut, the peat is left in piles to dry out before being used as fuel. Peat removal has been reintroduced in some nature reserves, to keep the water level up.

▲ Frogbit, an uncommon floating plant of undisturbed ponds and ditches in East Anglia. Its leaves are the shape of water-lily pads.

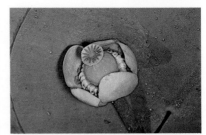

▲ Yellow Water-lily in fruit. Though tolerant of the polluted waters of the Broads, it is soon destroyed by disturbance from motorboats.

▲ Bladderwort (*left*), a rootless plant, feeds on water creatures which it traps in bladders on its submerged leaves. Water Violet (*centre*) also has submerged leaves, finely cut to offer least resistance to water movements. Purple Loosestrife (*right*) provides a fine display of colour along riverbanks in summer, often with Hemp Agrimony and Meadowsweet.

▼ The Marsh Pea (*left*) is not a common plant in Britain but it may be seen scrambling up reeds in East Anglia. The Arrowhead (*centre*) grows in shallow water. The Southern Marsh Orchid (*right*) favours damp alkaline areas like the Fens.

The Coast

The coast of East Anglia is often described as "flat and boring"; but its vast expanse of flatness is a paradise for wildlife. The wide, low-lying coastal belt, liable to floods, made it unattractive to early man and suitable only for grazing until recent decades, so today we are blessed with a heritage of unspoilt, wild and lonely country.

Sand dunes and shingle spits occur mainly along the Lincolnshire coast from the Humber to Gibraltar Point, and also along the North Norfolk coast from Hunstanton to the Broads, except for a 20-mile stretch of cliffs. Saltmarshes and mudflats often form behind dunes and spits, and these also occur extensively around the shores of the Wash and along the Essex shoreline.

Saltmarshes and Mudflats

About one quarter of Britain's total area of saltmarshes and mudflats are found in East Anglia. This is because its rivers drain over soft rather than hard rock and constantly bring down vast quantities of fine material. This is carried in suspension and, in the calmer waters of estuaries, is deposited as mobile mudflats.

This sticky, evil-smelling mud teems with burrowing and surface-dwelling invertebrates – food for fish and for many species of seabirds and waders. The long bills of Curlews, Godwits, Redshanks and Sandpipers are designed for probing deep in the mud for worms. Oystercatchers use their stout bills for opening molluscs, while Turnstones, with very short bills, select crustaceans under stones.

▲ East Mersea: mudscape, a familiar sight on East Anglian shores. The mud teems with life.

▼ The Ore estuary, the shingle spit deflecting its course out to sea; saltmarsh occurs behind.

▲ Black-tailed Godwits recently began to breed again in Britain, favouring damp East Anglian meadows for nesting. They winter on estuaries.

▲ The Common Seal is seen all round the East Anglian coast. It breeds mainly in the Wash.

▲ The Curlew Sandpiper, a rare winter visitor: its long bill probes the mud for marine worms.

▼ Oystercatchers use their strong bills to open molluscs found on the surface of the mud.

The surface of the mud is also covered with inconspicuous filamentous algae and the eel grasses, important food resources for wildfowl and geese. The Dark-breasted Brent Goose, for which the area is famous, feeds mainly on a species of eel grass. Other wildfowl which feed on the algae include Wigeon, Shelduck, Shoveler and Pintail. The Canada Goose, now well established in Britain, also moves to the estuaries in winter months.

Despite the low winter temperatures, the East Anglian flats rarely freeze in winter. They are therefore particularly important for enormous populations of overwintering wildfowl and waders, most of which return to their Arctic breeding grounds in the summer months. The East Anglian estuaries provide wintering grounds for an internationally significant proportion of many species of migratory birds.

The higher levels of the mudflats are first colonized by Cord-grass and species of Glasswort. These plants help to stabilize the mobile deposits and therefore allow other species from the saltmarsh plant community to colonize the mud between them.

▲ The Ringed Plover nests on sand or shingle. It is seen in winter on sandy and muddy shores.

▼ Knot and Godwits. In winter ducks and waders amass on East Anglia's food-rich mudflats.

▲ Shelduck feeding on surface algae on the estuarine flats. They usually nest in sandy burrows, often near estuaries or on dunes.

▲ Pintail (drake). This elegant species visits estuaries and coastal marshes in winter. It nests in fens, marshes and wet grazing land.

Few flowering plant species tolerate the fluctuating salinity and water levels on saltmarshes. Amongst those that can are some which put on a grand show during their flowering season – Thrift in June, Sea Lavender in August and Sea Aster in September.

The vegetation growing on the mud encourages more silt to be deposited around it. So the level of the marsh rises imperceptibly each year. This would normally result in the level rising out of reach of even the highest spring tides and terrestrial vegetation eventually taking over. In East Anglia however two factors usually prevent this.

One is the gradual submergence of the east coast by 30 cm per century, resulting in a balance between the building-up and erosion of the saltmarsh. The other is the presence of sea walls (man-made earth embankments) which have been built at the landward end of the saltmarsh. These sea walls, which extend around much of the East Anglian coast, interrupt the natural transition from saltmarsh to fully terrestial vegetation. The sea walls have been rebuilt and repaired throughout his-

▲ Scaup (drake). This diving duck is a winter visitor to Britain's estuaries and coastal waters.

▼ Blyth Marshes: low wooded cliffs offer fine vantage points across the coastal marshlands.

▲ Twenty per cent of the world's Brent Goose population over-winters in the Essex estuaries.

▼ The drab saltmarshes come alive in summer with the pinks and mauves of flowering plants.

tory in a successful attempt to create valu-able pasture land from saltmarsh.

Behind many of the sea walls, the land is still unimproved semi-natural marshland used only for summer grazing. This pro-vides an important refuge for many species of wildlife, including several plants which particularly favour these areas – such as Wild Celery, Water-plantain, Sea Club-rush and the attractive pink-flowering Marsh Mallows and Flower-ing Rushes. These marshlands provide retreats for waders forced off the shore by the high tide, grazing and nesting sites for our breeding ducks and geese, and hunt-ing ground for the Short-eared Owl.

Ditches (called dykes) help drain the marshy land in summer, when it is used as grazing pasture. The dykes remain water-filled in summer and provide refuges for a number of animals whose habitats else-where are diminishing. These include the Otter, Water Vole and species of butterfly. The Heron may often be seen fishing in the dykes.

The sea walls provide an excellent van-tage point for observing wildlife, and are often public rights of way.

▲ Aerial view of the Wash saltmarshes, riddled with natural drainage channels; the incoming tide sweeps rapidly up these creeks.

▲ Sea Lavender is abundant in East Anglia, where it covers the saltmarshes with a carpet of mauve in August.

▲ Cord-grass or Rice-grass, a rapid colonizer of the bare flats, helps stabilize the mud.

▲ Glasswort or Marsh Samphire is another colon-izer. Its succulent stems turn red in autumn.

▼ The Short-eared Owl may be seen hunting over marshes along the coast.

▼ Flowering Rush is one of the freshwater plants which find refuge in the coastal dykes.

Sand and Shingle

East Anglia's coast, apart from its muddy shores, is formed mainly of sand and shingle – favoured nesting sites for many coastal birds, in particular the Common and Little Terns, the Avocet, Ringed Plover and Black-headed Gull. These shores may also support an interesting array of plants. Neither sand nor shingle can easily retain the water necessary for plant life; this factor, together with strong coastal winds, salt spray and sunshine, means that many plants characteristic of this habitat have special features to cope with harsh conditions and limited water supply.

In many places the sand and shingle form spits and bars, a feature of the East Anglian coastline, especially in Suffolk and Norfolk. These are formed by waves striking the shore obliquely and driving the shore material along (a process called long shore drift). In some places shingle ridges occur in series, parallel with the shore. These are thrown up by waves during powerful storms.

▲ The Avocet now breeds only along the Suffolk coast where shallow brackish lagoons and muddy islands provide a suitable habitat.

▲ Havergate Island: Avocets returned to Britain in 1947 to breed here, after a century's absence.

▼ Gibraltar Point dunes: Marram Grass binds the sands against the eroding winter gales.

Extensive sand dunes are more characteristic of the west and north of Britain, but there are some in East Anglia, such as along the north Norfolk coast and at Saltfleetby in Lincolnshire. Sand dunes are formed by wind rather than wave action. Where extensive sand flats are exposed along the shore at low tide, the surface layers have a chance to dry out and thus become mobile in the onshore winds. Windblown sand accumulates around even tiny obstacles and thus an embryo dune develops. Once colonized by dune plants, such as Sea Rocket, this pioneer dune may eventually build up and become a permanent feature of the coast; new dunes will develop on the seaward side of it.

▲ Fulmars nest on sea cliffs; in East Anglia they breed only on the north Norfolk coast at Hunstanton and on the Weybourne Cliffs.

The familiar tussocks seen on sand dunes are Marram Grass. This helps to stabilize the shifting sands. The famous, though rare, colonizer of the shingle is the Sea Pea. Both these plants help with the retention of nutrients and water in the substrate.

The further back it is from the sea, the longer the vegetation has had to develop and the greater the variety of plants to be found. The more common flowers such as Bird's Foot Trefoil, Ragwort, Sea Campion, Biting Stonecrop and Rest-harrow create a colourful display. Chalk-loving species such as Viper's Bugloss and Wild Thyme may be found where shell fragments accumulate, and Lady's Bedstraw and the tiny Eyebrights may also be seen growing here.

▲ Black-headed Gulls nest colonially, sometimes in thousands, on dunes, shingle or marshes.

Further back from the sea, heathland or coastal scrub may develop and here Sea Buckthorn and Tamarisk may grow, restricting the growth of the attractive ground flora but providing food and shelter for birds on migration.

▲ Little Terns breed in small colonies on sand and shingle close to the high tide line.

▼ The Arctic Tern (*left*) can be seen in summer. Chalk-loving Pyramidal Orchids (*centre*) occur in dune slacks rich with shell fragments. Sea Buckthorn (*right*) dominates some older dunes.

▲ The Small Skipper finds refuge on the coast.

▲ Natterjack Toads live in pools in dune slacks.

▼ Plants of sand and shingle are adapted to cope with the lack of water and drying sun and wind.

▲ The rare Sea Pea (abundant in a few places on Suffolk shingle beaches) has a waxy surface covering the leaves to control water loss.

▲ Spring Whitlow-grass, like many plants of sand and shingle, completes its cycle before the summer dryness becomes intolerable.

▲ The hairy as well as waxy surface of the Yellow Horned Poppy helps cut down water loss.

▲ Biting Stonecrop has succulent stems for storing water. It is also called Wall Pepper.

▼ Sea Bindweed (*left*) and Sea Holly (*right*) are no longer common plants of the coast but their attractive flowers are still to be found in July and August on sandy and shingly shores.

Grassland

There are still small areas of grassland in East Anglia that have been left relatively undisturbed for many centuries. Grazing by animals, including rabbits, and also hay-cutting have prevented both the invasion of scrub and the dominance of the coarser grasses. Thus an ever-increasing wealth of flowering plants has been allowed to survive, producing the characteristically herb-rich ancient pasture, with its associated hum of insect life.

This rich semi-natural habitat has unfortunately suffered a serious decline over the last decade, owing to several different factors. Firstly much of this grassland has been converted during this century to agricultural land. Secondly grazing pasture, originally meadows, has been "improved" by the addition of fertilizers to encourage one or two species of grasses or clover. Also, the decline of the rabbit population through myxomatosis has meant that the coarser grasses and scrub tend to invade where once they were kept down by rabbit grazing.

▲ Male Common Blue Butterfly (female is darker and browner). It is seen in open grassy places. The larvae feed on plants like clovers.

▲ The Small Copper is seen in grassy fields from May sometimes right through to October. The larvae feed on sorrel.

▼ Poppies in a Suffolk wheat field: annuals do well in regularly ploughed land, but the use of herbicides has made this sight a rare one.

The exquisite flora of chalk and lime-stone – including Rockrose, Squinancy-wort, Horseshoe Vetch, Salad Burnet, Quaking Grass, Wild Thyme, Dropwort and Clustered Bellflower – now exist in only a few sites. These sites tend to be located on steep unploughable slopes, such as those along the Devil's Dyke in Cambridgeshire, and patches in the Lin-colnshire Wolds and at the southern end of Lincolnshire's limestone cliff. All the plant species mentioned above are faithful to chalk and limestone soils, and are a good indication of soil type where they grow. Rarities like the silky Pasque Flower, Bee and Pyramidal Orchids, and Spiked Speedwell, are occasionally found with other chalk-loving species.

Few areas of ancient pasture have sur-vived on the more neutral soils of the boul-der clays. Of those that have, some are protected in reserves, such as the Suffolk Fritillary meadows, where each year dur-ing spring the rare Fritillaries bloom in thousands (see below). More common plants of undisturbed grassland are Cows-lips and Small Scabious.

There are also many largely overlooked stretches of grassland such as those flank-ing the roadsides. These verges are rich in flowering plants, and the County Council cutting programmes are sometimes timed so that the plants can set seed first. The Sulphur Clover, a characteristic plant of the verges, is restricted to East Anglia.

Some disused railway tracks are now managed as reserves or nature trails, and are well worth a visit. The rich grassland with patches of scrub provides habitats for large numbers of small mammals – ideal hunting ground for the Kestrel.

Churchyards and the land surrounding ancient monuments can be a haven in an otherwise agricultural landscape. As long as the grass is not closely mown, nor the area totally unmanaged and allowed to become overgrown by shrubs and bram-bles, the grassland between the ancient stones will remain enriched with many colourful flowers.

▼ The Fritillary, whose strange flowers range from dull purple to a creamy white, grows in undis-turbed damp meadows. This sensitive species, which was once far more widespread, has been drastically reduced by the ploughing up of ancient meadows, and is now restricted to a few areas, including some in Suffolk.

▲ The Pasque Flower: its British distribution is very restricted, but it can be found on the Cambridgeshire and Lincolnshire chalk and limestone, especially on ancient earthworks.

▼ Fritillary meadows: fine displays of beautiful Fritillaries can be seen flowering in mid-May, pro-tected in Suffolk reserves.

▲ The lovely Cowslip, once common, has suffered not only from the ploughing up of pastures but also from over-picking by wine-makers.

▲ Skylarks, birds of open country where "song-posts" are lacking, combine their warbling song with an aerial display – the "song-flight".

▲ Sulphur Clover, restricted in Britain to East Anglia, can often be seen flanking the roadsides. It is characteristic of boulder clays.

▲ Meadow Saxifrage, a lowland saxifrage (most are mountain species), is found more commonly in East Anglia than in other parts of Britain.

▼ A Suffolk churchyard in May with Meadow Saxifrage in bloom: churchyards, if neither closely mown nor neglected, will remain full of flowers.

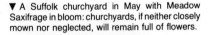

▼ Green-winged Orchid: one of the many species which find a refuge in churchyards – wildlife havens in an agricultural landscape.

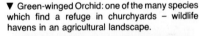

Heathland

Heathlands, which cover quite large tracts of East Anglia, turn into a carpet of purple heather in the summer. Heather, like other heathland plants, is well adapted to poor, acid soils. Where the soil is dry, Bell Heather dominates, but where it is wet, Cross-leaved Heath is the dominant species. The Suffolk Sandlings, Sandringham Estate, Tiptree Heath and much of the Breckland (see next page) are good examples of heathland areas.

The poor heathland soil contains few nutrients but Gorse flourishes there, as do other members of the pea family like Bird's Foot Trefoil. This is because they use bacteria in their roots to obtain nitrogen (an important plant nutrient) directly from the air in the soil.

The heathland soil is acid and supports a small assemblage of herbaceous species such as Heath Bedstraw, Storksbill, Tormentil and Wood Sage, which are unable to grow on alkaline, chalky soils. Plants with such strict requirements provide us with an immediate indication of what soil conditions are like in the areas in which they prosper.

Characteristic heathland birds are the well-camouflaged Nightjar, Stonechat, and also the Red-backed Shrike, whose main British breeding ground is in East Anglia and the New Forest.

Woodland may encroach into heathland which is not intensively grazed by sheep or by rabbits; Birch and Pine trees are the primary invaders.

▲ The Nightjar, a well-camouflaged summer visitor from Africa, nests on open ground. It flies at night to catch insects in its gaping mouth.

▲ The Red-backed Shrike, a summer visitor to East Anglia, nests in thorny thickets and frequents heathland.

▼ Heathlands are characterized by the dominance of dwarf shrubs, especially the heathers.

▼ Bell Heather (*right*) and Ling (*left*) flower in August. Look out too for Cross-leaved Heath.

Breckland

This unique corner of Britain, which straddles the western end of the Norfolk-Suffolk border, is fundamentally heathland with dry sandy soil that is easily blown away if vegetation is removed. The features characterizing Breckland as opposed to ordinary heathland are due chiefly to its geology and climate and also its history.

The chief *geological* feature of the area is the predominant covering of wind-blown glacial sand which is of varying thickness, and even non-existent in some areas. This means that the underlying chalk reaches the surface in places, thus affecting the vegetation; here the characteristically chalk-loving plants may be found (see Grassland, page 24). Plants of chalk grassland and heathland are found intermixed where the sand layer is very thin; a strange feature of the Breckland is to find plants which will not tolerate chalky soil growing with those which thrive on it.

The Breckland *climate* is similar to a continental one – with hot summers, cold winters and low annual rainfall. This is because it lies too far from the west coast to be affected by the warm, moist Atlantic and yet not near enough the North Sea to be strongly affected by its ameliorating conditions. Its very well-drained soil tends to exaggerate the effects of the dry climate, such that many common plant species are unable to survive.

Continental species however, such as Sand and Spanish Catchflies, Spring Speedwell and Maiden Pink, find that conditions in the Breckland are more favourable than anywhere else in Britain.

Historically, the area was one of the first in East Anglia to be cleared by man, and there is evidence of a sparse though almost continuous occupation throughout history. Man introduced sheep and rabbits which, through overgrazing, caused expanses of bare sand to remain unvegetated. Some of these areas are conserved in this state to protect the rare species of plants that thrive there. The Stone Curlew, now a rare bird, was, earlier this century, extremely common in the Breckland since it selects nesting sites on dry, sparsely vegetated heathland. Recent historical events, especially the extensive planting of conifers by the Forestry Commission, have altered the character of a large part of the Breckland (see page 32).

▼ Langmere: one of a number of Breckland meres (bodies of water which dry up in summer).

▲ Maiden Pink (*left*) may be found on the more acid, sandy soils, whereas Purple Milkvetch (*centre*) is found in lime-rich soils where chalk is near the surface. Spanish Catchfly (*right*) like the Sand Catchfly below, grows in sandy soils; both can be seen in Breckland roadside verges.

▲ The tricoloured Wild Pansy of the Breck is the same sub-species that is found in coastal dunes – reflecting a similarity in habitat.

▲ Sand Catchfly, like the Spanish Catchfly, is in Britain virtually confined to the Breck.

▼ Breckland scene: Stone Curlew and the Mossy Stonecrop favour the bare shifting sandy soils, which however soon become stabilized by Sand Sedge and the recent conifer plantations.

Stone Curlew

Gorse

Sand Sedge

Mossy Stonecrop

Woodland

In a country where woodland is the natural dominant vegetation, it is perhaps sad to find that less than six per cent of East Anglia is still under forest cover, and that much of that is recent coniferous plantation. Once again we find, as in so many habitats, that traditional management encourages the greatest variety of wildlife: unmanaged woods tend to become dark and lifeless. Fortunately in East Anglia some coppice woods and wood pasture are still maintained.

Coppice Woods

A coppiced tree, rather than having just one trunk, has several slender poles growing from ground level. Coppice woods consist of stands of trees of different ages, each of which is felled to the ground on a rotational system once every 10–20 years, after which several shoots will spring up again from the stump: no replanting is therefore necessary.

In recently coppiced stands, light is plentiful, and there develops a tangled jungle of summer-flowering plants, such as Bugle, Water Avens, Red Campion and some species of orchid.

The canopy of older stands of trees, however, casts such a dense shade that very few herb species can survive. But early in the year, before the canopy develops, spring-flowering species are able to flourish, especially since there is no competition from the host of summer plants of open ground. In spring therefore the woodland floor becomes a carpet of colour, with Bluebells, Wood Anemones, Primroses, or Oxlips (a rare relative of the Cowslip whose British range is confined to East Anglia). Other spring woodland flowers include Lesser Celandine, Violet, Bittercress and Herb Paris.

The variety of plants in the young stands is matched in the sunny glades and rides, where trampling and grazing tend to maintain a shorter turf, allowing smaller plants like Yellow Pimpernel to receive light.

The rich variety of flowers found in coppice woods, unsurpassed in other types of woodland, supports a wealth of insect life, notably butterflies like the Grizzled Skipper, the Fritillaries and the Comma.

The dense thickets of middle-aged coppices are valuable nesting areas for many passerines, such as the Nightingale and various tits and warblers. This is due to the absence of comparable nesting sites elsewhere, and also to the wealth of insect life. Small mammals are able to find plenty of foodstuffs within the safety of woods. Deer are usually controlled because they cause damage to young coppiced shoots.

▼ A coppice wood in spring. As the poles grow their canopies cast too much shade for summer flowers. Only spring flowers like these Bluebells receive sufficient light to flourish.

▲ The Comma butterfly (*left*) may be seen along the flowery woodland rides, margins and glades. Hedgehogs (*centre*) live in woods and hedgerows. The Nightingale (*right*) returns each spring from Africa to the same wood, where it selects nesting sites in the dense scrub of eight-year-old coppices rather than mature woods.

▲ Spring flowers of deciduous woods: Bluebells (*left*) and the more local Oxlip (*centre*) may form a carpet of colour. The Oxlip is restricted in Britain to East Anglian woodlands on chalky boulder clays. Sweet Violet (*right*): violets may also grow in profusion on woodland floors.

▼ Summer flowers flourish in the lighter areas of woods where coppicing has opened up the canopy. Water Avens (*left*) grows in damp places. The Military Orchid (*centre*) is restricted in Britain to a few areas, including one Suffolk reserve. The Early Purple Orchid (*right*) is more widespread.

Wood Pasture

The traditional Royal Forests, like Epping and Hatfield, and the deer parks and commonlands, provide not only timber but also pasture for grazing. Several species of deer, especially Fallow Deer, are not uncommon in these habitats, and so coppicing is not feasible because of grazing damage to young coppiced shoots.

Some trees (pollards) are therefore cut back (or pollarded) to a height out of reach of deer. At this height, several branches will then develop, just as coppiced trees do from the base. Other trees (standards) are allowed to mature naturally. Pollards and standards provide timber for different purposes – pollards for fencing panels and basketwork, and standards for planks intended for larger items.

The old pollards contain much dead wood – food for many types of beetles and woodlice, which in turn provide food for Woodpeckers, the Nuthatch and the Treecreeper. Tawny Owls and Jays also nest in the pollards.

Wood pasture is generally broken up by large grazing plains of grass or heath. These plains receive plenty of light and hence, like the coppice woods, support a rich flora. Plants commonly found growing here are Red and White Campion, St John's Wort and the Willowherbs.

Thus open areas occur alongside woodland, which will regenerate wherever grazing pressure is low; such well-managed wood pasture provides a great variety of habitats. The diversity will be maintained only as long as the land is used in the traditional way.

▲ Old pollarded oak, with huge crown; trees of wood pasture or parkland can be ancient.

▼ Tawny Owls may roost in the sturdy crowns of pollards, and nest in the ancient trunks.

▼ Ixworth Park: traditional parkland provides a wealth of habitats as well as timber and grazing.

▼ Fallow Deer: this is now the most widespread species in deer parks in East Anglia.

Hedgerows

East Anglia, perhaps more than any other region in Britain, has suffered the destruction not only of its woodland but also its hedgerows. In some areas the remaining hedgerows are the sole havens for woodland plants for many miles.

The hedgerows also provide secluded routeways for shy animals, linking patches of wood and scrub. Hedgehogs, mice and voles may be seen amongst the vegetation. Some species of birds have adapted well to the comparatively new agricultural landscape, but most of these rely considerably on hedgerows (in the absence of woodland) for food and nesting sites. Yellowhammer, Whitethroat, Corn Bunting, Chaffinch and Dunnock may be seen and heard amongst the scrub, and Partridges nest at the base. Hedgerows can sometimes be more rewarding for sheer numbers of species to be spotted than a nature reserve.

Long-established hedges, compared with newly planted ones, contain a greater variety of trees and shrubs including Hazel, Dogwood, Spindle and Wayfaring Tree, and are richer in wildlife. It is possible to judge the approximate age of a hedge in East Anglia by the number of tree species in a 30-yard stretch, adding one century for every species growing there. It is not unusual along some of the quiet lanes to find 900-year-old hedges which have survived alongside man's ever-changing world.

Plantations

Most coniferous forests in Britain are located on the poorer sandy soils, and replace heathland. Some are planted in place of ancient woodland. They are in some ways comparable to fields of corn. Like a cornfield, they are established by organized planting, and contain trees of the same age and usually of the same species (generally conifers). They are eventually completely cleared by felling and the area is then replanted.

The crowded growth of evergreen trees, which produce a deep acid litter of needles, does not favour the rich and varied ground flora characteristic of other woodland types, except along rides and firebreaks. But there is no lack of interest here for the naturalist. Many species of birds are well-suited to these forest plantations: for example the Lesser Redpoll, Crossbill, Goldcrest, Coal Tit and Nightjar.

Some of East Anglia's coniferous forests are safe strongholds for the Red Squirrel, whose British distribution is sadly declining. The large expanse of conifer plantation known as Thetford Chase in the Breck now claims the finest Red Deer in Britain.

▲ The Red Squirrel still has a stronghold in East Anglia, despite its decline elsewhere in Britain. It favours coniferous forests, feeding on pine seeds, toadstools and other fruits.

▼ The Crossbill feeds on coniferous seeds, and nests in January when food supply is at a peak.

▼ Red Deer reach their maximum size in Britain in the sheltered East Anglian forests.

Common Species of the Countryside and Seashore

Some of Britain's animals and plants can be found only in certain regions, or are more easily found in some areas than in others. Living alongside these rare or local species are, of course, many animals and plants which are fairly widespread throughout the country. The more common species of British birds, wild flowers, trees, butterflies, mammals and seashore animals are illustrated on the following pages. These illustrations form a basic field guide to the majority of the regions in Britain.

The captions to the bird illustrations indicate the bird's usual haunts, and if it is seen only in certain seasons, this fact is mentioned. Measurements indicate the size of the bird from the tip of the beak to the end of the tail. Notes to aid identification of the species are also included.

The mammals that are illustrated are accompanied by captions which indicate their average size. Those for hoofed mammals indicate their height at the shoulder. Others indicate the length of their bodies from nose to rump. The captions also give an indication as to when the animal is most active and therefore most easily observed.

The wild flowers are grouped according to their commonest colours; their most frequently used names are given in the captions, along with their habitats, the months in which they flower and their height or the length of creeping stems if they grow horizontally.

The illustrations of butterflies frequently show them on the plants they prefer to visit. The captions indicate the butterflies' usual habitats, the months when they are most frequently seen, and their wingspan.

Information about the sizes of the seashore animals are detailed in their captions, while the height of the trees is given on page 96. Selected identifying characteristics are given in the captions to the trees.

A hedgerow in early summer—one of the countryside's most rewarding habitats, since it shelters a wide variety of species. This illustration features some of the common, widespread plants and animals included in the following pages.

Birds

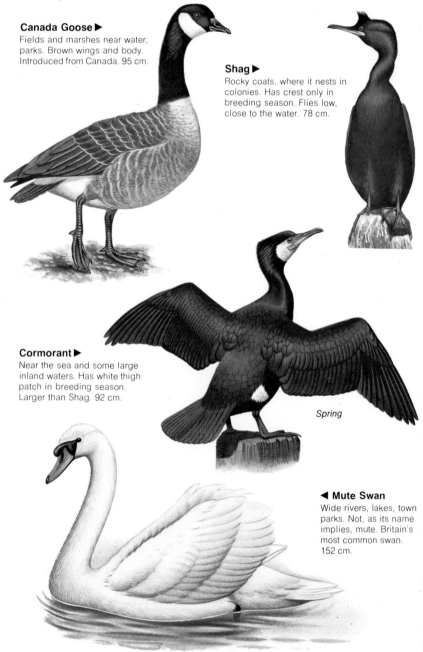

Canada Goose ▶
Fields and marshes near water; parks. Brown wings and body. Introduced from Canada. 95 cm.

Shag ▶
Rocky coats, where it nests in colonies. Has crest only in breeding season. Flies low, close to the water. 78 cm.

Cormorant ▶
Near the sea and some large inland waters. Has white thigh patch in breeding season. Larger than Shag. 92 cm.

Spring

◀ Mute Swan
Wide rivers, lakes, town parks. Not, as its name implies, mute. Britain's most common swan. 152 cm.

35

▼ Wigeon
Near sea, especially in winter; lakes and marshes. Seen August-April; a few stay to breed. 46 cm.

Mallard ▲
Inland waters and estuaries. Purplish-blue wing patch seen in flight. 58 cm.

◄ Pintail
Lakes and marshes, near coast in winter. Pointed tail and long, elegant neck. Seen September-March; a few stay to breed. 66 cm.

Shoveler ►
Quiet lakes and shallow water. Large, heavy bill. Pale blue forewings of both male and female show in flight. 51 cm.

▼ Teal
Inland waters and estuaries. The smallest duck in Britain. Dark bill. Quick and agile in flight. 35 cm.

▲ Tufted Duck
Lakes, ponds, gravel pits and parks. Dumpy, active diving duck. Note female's yellow eye. 43 cm.

36

▼ Pochard
Lakes and backwaters. In flight, both sexes have dark wings with páler grey central bar. 46 cm.

▲ Shelduck
Coasts and estuaries, often in flocks; also large inland lakes. Female has no red knob on bill. 61 cm.

▲ Red-breasted Merganser
Coastal areas; wooded lakes, rivers, in breeding season. 58 cm.

Grey Heron ▶
Near water: rivers, lakes and seashores. Head is drawn back in flight. 92 cm.

Summer

Winter

▼ Little Grebe
Inland waters. Secretive and hard to spot. 27 cm.

▲ Great Crested Grebe
Inland waters, sometimes on sea in winter. 48 cm.

Winter

Summer

Buzzard ▼
Often seen soaring over moors and farmland. Rare in east and south-east England. 54 cm.

▼ Kestrel
Moors, coasts, farmland; some nest in towns. Hovers when hunting. 34 cm.

Coot ▶
Lakes, reservoirs, open water. Larger, heavier bird than Moorhen. 38 cm.

▲ Moorhen
Ponds, lakes and streams. 33 cm.

◀ Partridge
Farmland, moors. Small head, short tail and legs. Often in small groups. 30 cm.

♂

▼ Pheasant
Farmland, scrub, woodland. Males can have white neckring. Male 87 cm, female 58 cm.

♀

◀ Redshank
Seashores and wet
meadows. Probes in
mud. 28 cm.

Summer

Winter

▼ Oystercatcher
Seashores, estuaries. Often
in groups. White band on
throat in winter. 43 cm.

▲ Turnstone
Shingle or rocky coasts. Turns over stones,
seaweed, to find food. 23 cm.

Common Sandpiper ▲
Rivers, streams and lakes.
Seen April-October; a few in
winter. 20 cm.

▼ Ringed Plover
Sandy and muddy shores.
In summer, white wing bar
shows in flight. 19 cm.

*Adult in
summer*

Juvenile

Lapwing ▲
Farmland, marshes, mudflats. 30 cm.

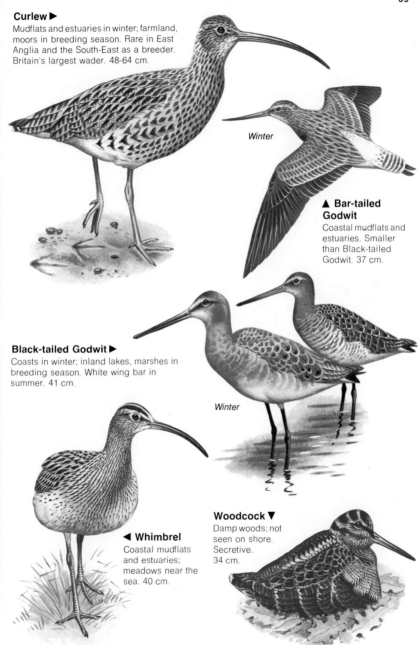

Curlew ▶
Mudflats and estuaries in winter; farmland, moors in breeding season. Rare in East Anglia and the South-East as a breeder. Britain's largest wader. 48-64 cm.

Winter

▲ Bar-tailed Godwit
Coastal mudflats and estuaries. Smaller than Black-tailed Godwit. 37 cm.

Black-tailed Godwit ▶
Coasts in winter; inland lakes, marshes in breeding season. White wing bar in summer. 41 cm.

Winter

◀ Whimbrel
Coastal mudflats and estuaries; meadows near the sea. 40 cm.

Woodcock ▼
Damp woods; not seen on shore. Secretive. 34 cm.

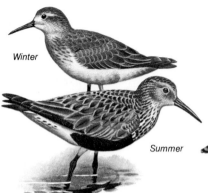

Winter

Summer

▲ Dunlin

Mudflats and estuaries. Common winter
shorebird; less common in summer. 19 cm.

Winter

▲ Sanderling

Sandy shores along coasts. Seen
August-May. Short, straight beak. 20 cm.

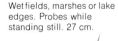

Snipe ▼

Wet fields, marshes or lake
edges. Probes while
standing still. 27 cm.

Greenshank ▼

Coasts, marshes. Seen chiefly on
migration. Some breed in Scotland. 30 cm.

▼ Knot

Sand or mudflats in
estuaries. Larger than
Dunlin. Seen mostly
August-May. 25 cm.

Summer

♂

◄ Ruff

Marshes, wet
meadows, edges
of reservoirs.
Seen mostly in
spring and
autumn. 29 cm.

♂

Winter

Winter

▼ Common Tern
Near sea; also nests inland in Scotland.
Seen April-October. 34 cm.

Summer

◄ Little Tern
Shingle beaches. Never
has full black cap like other
terns. Seen
April-September. 24 cm.

Summer

Herring Gull ▼
Coastal ports and seaside
towns. Wingtips are black
with white spots. 56 cm.

Summer

◄ Black-headed Gull
Inland and near the sea. Dark
brown "hood" in summer
only. 37 cm.

Summer

Common Gull ►
Coasts; often inland in
winter. Smaller and
less widespread than
Herring Gull. 41 cm.

Lesser Black-backed Gull ►
Coasts and inland.
Mainly a summer
visitor. 53 cm.

▼ Guillemot
Rocky coasts. Neck and throat are white in winter. Seen at cliff sites December-August. 42 cm.

◄ Fulmar
Rocky coasts. Nests on cliffs. Always sits, never stands. Mostly out at sea in winter. 47 cm.

Puffin ►
Rocky islands and sea cliffs. Colourful bill in summer. 30 cm.

Summer

Summer

▼ Collared Dove
Large gardens, parks and farmland. Long white tail with black base. 30 cm

◄ Stock Dove
Woods and cliffs; sometimes in towns. Darker, smaller bird than Woodpigeon. 33 cm.

Rock Dove ▼
Coasts, usually on sea cliffs. Town pigeons are descended from these birds. 33 cm.

Woodpigeon ►
Farmland, woods and towns. White neck patch on adult. 41 cm.

▼ Short-eared Owl
Open country. Hunts in day-time or at dusk. 37 cm.

◄ Barn Owl
Open country, especially farmland. Mostly nocturnal. 34 cm.

Little Owl ▼
Farmland and wooded country. Underside is streaked. Often seen in daylight. 22 cm.

◄ Long-eared Owl
Edges of woods. Underside all dark. Nocturnal. 34 cm.

▲ Tawny Owl
Parks, woodland and farmland; sometimes towns. Large head. Nocturnal. 38 cm.

◄ Kingfisher
Near rivers and lakes; seashore in winter. Dives from low perch or from a hover. 17 cm.

▼ Cuckoo
Anywhere in countryside. Male's song is well known. April-September. 30 cm.

Swift ▶
Breeds mainly in towns;
may fly over countryside.
Seen end of April-
August/September. 17 cm.

▼ Sand Martin
Banks and sandy cliffs. Seen
April-September. 12 cm.

◀ House Martin
Suburban areas and
countryside. Seen
April-October.
13 cm.

◀ Swallow
Farms and open country;
often near water. Seen
April-September/October.
19 cm.

**◀ Great Spotted
Woodpecker**
Woodlands. Large
white patches on
wings. 23 cm.

**◀ Green
Woodpecker**
Deciduous woods,
parks. Yellow-green
rump seen in flight.
Rare in Scotland.
32 cm.

**Lesser Spotted
Woodpecker ▶**
Deciduous woods,
parks. Not in
Scotland.
Sparrow-sized.
14 cm.

▼ Dunnock
Bushes and shrubs everywhere.
Slender bill, unlike sparrows. 14.5 cm.

▲ Meadow Pipit
Upland moors and other open areas. .
Smaller, daintier than larks. 14.5 cm.

Tree Pipit ▲
Heaths and areas with
scattered trees. Seen
April-September. 15 cm.

**◄ Yellow
Wagtail**
Grassy places
near water.
Seen April-late
September.
17 cm.

♂

▲ Skylark
Open country, especially farmland.
Rises vertically to a great height in song
flight. 18 cm.

♂

Summer

◄ Grey Wagtail
By lochs or
fast-flowing hill
steams;
waterfalls in
lowlands. 18 cm.

▲ Pied Wagtail
Towns and countryside, usually near
water. Females are greyer. Takes insects
from the ground or the air. 18 cm.

▼ Willow Warbler
Gardens, woods and hedgerows. Flatter head and longer tail than Chiffchaff. Seen April–September. 11 cm.

▲ Sedge Warbler
Thick vegetation near water. Broad, pale stripe over eye. Seen April–September. 13 cm.

Wren ▶
Towns and countryside. Tiny, rotund bird with cocked tail. 9.5 cm.

Reed Warbler ▼
Reed beds. Not in Scotland. Seen April–September. 13 cm.

♂

♀

▲ Blackcap
Wooded areas. Seen April–September, a few in winter. 14 cm.

▼ Whitethroat
Thick, low bushes. Seen April–September. 14 cm.

▲ Garden Warbler
Hedges or woods with thick undergrowth. Seen April–September. 14 cm.

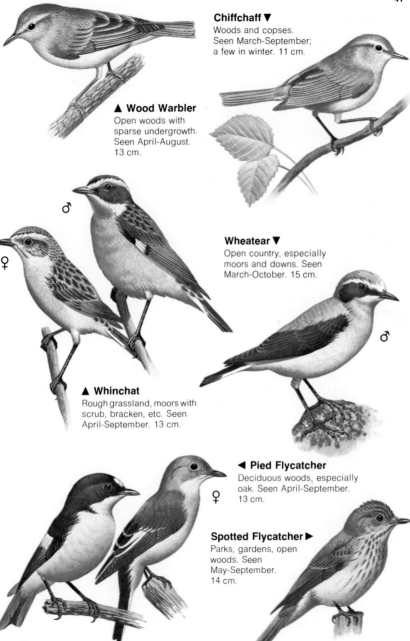

Chiffchaff ▼
Woods and copses.
Seen March-September;
a few in winter. 11 cm.

▲ Wood Warbler
Open woods with
sparse undergrowth.
Seen April-August.
13 cm.

♂

♀

Wheatear ▼
Open country, especially
moors and downs. Seen
March-October. 15 cm.

♂

▲ Whinchat
Rough grassland, moors with
scrub, bracken, etc. Seen
April-September. 13 cm.

◄ Pied Flycatcher
Deciduous woods, especially
oak. Seen April-September.
♀ 13 cm.

Spotted Flycatcher ▶
Parks, gardens, open
woods. Seen
May-September.
14 cm.

Blackbird ▼
In trees and bushes everywhere. Young are paler than female with breast more strongly spotted. 25 cm.

♀

♂

▼ Starling
Most places, including cities. In summer, has purple and green gloss and mostly yellow bill. 22 cm.

Juvenile

Adult in winter

▲ Redwing
Farmland, commons and other open areas. A few breed in Scotland. Seen October–April. 21 cm.

◄ Fieldfare
Farmland, orchards, open areas. White underwings. Seen October–April. 25.5 cm.

▼ Redstart
Heaths, parks, open woods. Seen April–September. Rather Robin-like. 14 cm.

♀

♂

Robin ▲
Gardens, hedgerows and woodland. Juvenile is spotted, without any red. 14 cm.

◄ Song Thrush
Trees and bushes in towns and country.
Smashes snails on stones. 23 cm.

Long-tailed Tit ►
Hedgerows and
woodland edges.
14 cm. (7.5 cm of
which is the tail).

◄ Great Tit
Gardens and
woodlands. Black
band on chest. 14 cm.

◄ Blue Tit
Woods and gardens.
Dark line on belly.
11 cm.

▲ Mistle Thrush
Woodland and open areas.
Larger than Blackbird; paler,
greyer than Song Thrush. 27 cm.

▼ Marsh Tit
Deciduous woods;
infrequently in
gardens. 11 cm.

▲ Coal Tit
Coniferous woods, parks,
gardens. Oblong white patch
on nape. 11 cm.

▼ Chaffinch
Farmland, hedgerows and woodland. Male is duller in winter. White wing bar seen in flght. 15 cm.

♀

♂

♀

♂

Summer

▲ Siskin
Usually coniferous woods in summer; birch, alder woods, sometimes gardens, in winter. 11 cm.

▲ Nuthatch
Deciduous wood and parks. Can descend trees head-first. Very short tail. Rare in Scotland. 14 cm.

▲ Hawfinch
Deciduous woodland, orchards. Very elusive. Big head and massive, broad bill. 16 cm.

◀ Treecreeper
Woodland, sometimes parks and gardens. Creeps up tree trunks using tail as support. 13 cm.

▲ Goldfinch
Open country, orchards and gardens. Distinctive broad yellow band across black wing. 12 cm.

▲ Bullfinch
Deciduous woodlands, hedges, orchards, gardens. Whitish wing bar on black wing. 15 cm.

Spring

◀ Linnet
Heathland and farmland. Forms large flocks in autumn on fields and waste ground. 13 cm.

▼ Lesser Redpoll
Coniferous and birch woods. Male has pink breast in spring. Streaked flanks (unlike Linnet). 12 cm.

▲ Greenfinch
Hedgerows, parks and gardens. Forages in flocks from autumn to spring. 15 cm.

▲ House Sparrow
Near houses in cities; on farms in the country. Distinctive black bib on male. 15 cm.

▼ Tree Sparrow
Farmland. White cheeks with black spot. Sometimes flocks with House Sparrow in winter. 14 cm.

▲ Corn Bunting
Open country, especially cornfields. Bigger than other buntings and finches. 18 cm.

▲ Yellowhammer
Farmland, heaths, young plantations. Flocks forage in fields in winter. Rare in Wales. 17 cm.

▲ Goldcrest
Large gardens and woods, especially conifers. Smallest British bird. 9 cm.

▲ Reed Bunting
Vegetation near water; may visit bird tables in winter. Male has less black on head in winter. 15 cm.

Carrion Crow ▶
Open country, town, along coasts. Usually seen alone, in pairs or small groups. 47 cm.

▼ Jay
Woodlands, parks and gardens. White rump and blue wing flash show in flight. 32 cm.

◀ Magpie
Hedgerows, farmland, scrub. Large black and white bird. Long, slender tail. 46 cm.

▼ Jackdaw
Cliffs, farmland and towns. Small black and grey crow. Forms large flocks. 33 cm.

▲ Rook
Farmland, open copses, villages. Forms large flocks. Baggy thighs. Bare whitish face in adults. 46 cm.

Mammals

▼ **Red Fox**
Farmland and woods, sometimes mountains and towns. Mainly nocturnal. 65 cm.

▲ **Badger**
Woods, sometimes mountains. Nocturnal. Can stay underground for several days in cold weather without food. 80 cm.

▼ **Roe Deer**
Conifer plantations, especially near water. Mainly nocturnal; hides during day. 70 cm.

▲ **Hedgehog**
Hedgerows, ditches, parks, gardens and moorland. Mainly nocturnal. 25 cm. .

▲ **Mole**
Underground in most kinds of soil in farmland, woods. Lives alone. Can swim well. 13 cm.

▼ Grey Squirrel
Woods, parks and gardens.
Introduced from N. America.
Diurnal. 27 cm.

Red Squirrel ▲
Mainly conifer woods. Partly replaced
by Grey Squirrel in England. 23 cm.

▼ Rabbit
Farmland, woodland, sand
dunes and hillsides. Active
at dusk and dawn. 40 cm.

◄ Brown Hare
Open farmland and
woodland. Mainly
nocturnal, but can often be
seen in day. 58 cm.

▼ Wood Mouse
Gardens,
hedgerows,
woods. Mainly
nocturnal. 9 cm.

▼ Common Shrew
Rough pasture, woods,
hedgerows, dunes and
marshes. Active day and
night. 7 cm.

▼ Short-tailed Vole
Open ground with
rough grass. Most
active at night; also
seen in day. 11 cm.

◀ Grey Seal
Rocky shores, mainly along Atlantic coast; some on east coast of Scotland and north-east coast of England. 3 m.

Common Seal ▶
Flat shores, estuaries and mudbanks on Scottish coasts and mainly east coast of England. Blunter head than Grey Seal. 1.5 m.

◀ Stoat
Woods, farmland, mountains. Tip of tail always black. Mainly nocturnal. 28 cm.

▲ Weasel
Same habitat as Stoat, but prefers dry places. Mainly nocturnal. 20 cm.

Water Vole ▶
Ponds, canals, streams and marshes. Mainly diurnal. May also be black. 19 cm.

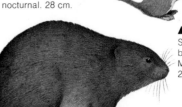

Otter ▶
Alongside rivers, lakes; marshes, coasts and the sea. Nocturnal. More common in Scotland. 70 cm.

Wild Flowers

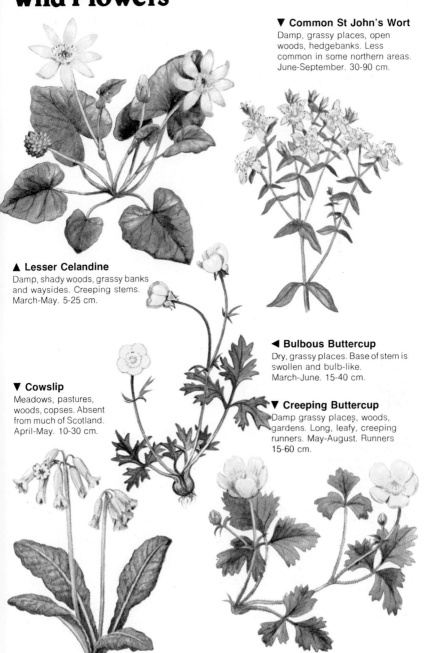

▼ Common St John's Wort
Damp, grassy places, open
woods, hedgebanks. Less
common in some northern areas.
June-September. 30-90 cm.

▲ Lesser Celandine
Damp, shady woods, grassy banks
and waysides. Creeping stems.
March-May. 5-25 cm.

◄ Bulbous Buttercup
Dry, grassy places. Base of stem is
swollen and bulb-like.
March-June. 15-40 cm.

▼ Cowslip
Meadows, pastures,
woods, copses. Absent
from much of Scotland.
April-May. 10-30 cm.

▼ Creeping Buttercup
Damp grassy places, woods,
gardens. Long, leafy, creeping
runners. May-August. Runners
15-60 cm.

▼ Creeping Jenny
Grassy, shady places; damp meadows, woods, under hedges. Rare in northern Scotland. June-August. Stems up to 60 cm.

◄ Yellow Rattle
Waysides and other grassy places. Seeds rattle inside ripe capsule. May-August. 12-40 cm.

Common Rockrose ►
Grassy, rocky places. Not a rose. Leaves are hairy.
May-September 5-30 cm.

Aaron's Rod ►
Banks, waste places, open scrub. Rarer in Scotland. June-August. 30-200 cm.

◄ Groundsel
Waste places; a
common garden weed.
Flowers all year round.
8-45 cm.

▲ Primrose
Woods, hedges and fields. Rarer
in the North. February-May.
8-15 cm.

◄ Herb Bennet
Woods, hedges, shady places.
Fruits are hooked. June-August.
20-60 cm.

◄ Broom
Heaths, waste ground,
open woods,
scrubland. May-June.
60-200 cm.

▲ Yellow Pimpernel
Woods and shady
hedgebanks. May-September.
Trailing stems up to 40 cm long.

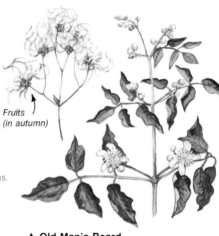

*Fruits
(in autumn)*

◀ Silverweed
Hedgebanks, grassy
places. Creeping stems.
May-August.

▲ Old Man's Beard
Woodland edges, hedgerows, scrub.
Rare in Scotland and northern
England. July-August. Up to 30 m.

▼ Bird's Foot Trefoil
Open, grassy places. Very long,
creeping stems. Pods look like a
bird's foot. May-June.

Golden Rod ▶
Woods, cliffs, hedges. Rarer
in the South-East.
July-September. 5-75 cm.

**▼ Creeping
Cinquefoil**
Hedgebanks, grassy
places. Creeping
stems. May-August.

▼ Ragwort
Roadsides, waste ground, grassy places. Flowerheads in flat-topped clusters. June-October. 30-150 cm

▲ Dandelion
Open grassy places and waste ground. March-October. 15-30 cm.

Rape ▶
Roadsides and fields. May-August. Up to 1m.

▼ Gorse
Heaths and commons. March-July. 60-200 cm.

▲ Wild Pansy
Grassy places and cornfields. Flowers can also be all yellow, all violet, or pink and white. April-September. 15-45 cm.

▼ Viper's Bugloss
Waysides and sand dunes. Sharp
hairs on stems. Bristly leaves. Rare in
Scotland. June-September. 30-90 cm.

Common
Forget-me-Not ▶
Roadsides, fields, and
open grassy places.
April-September.
15-30 cm.

◀ Sea Aster
Saltmarshes. Petals can
also be white.
July-October. 1 m.

◀ Common
Speedwell
Grassy places and
woods. May-August.
10-40 cm.

Common Milkwort ▶
Heaths, dunes, grassy
places. May-September.
10-30 cm.

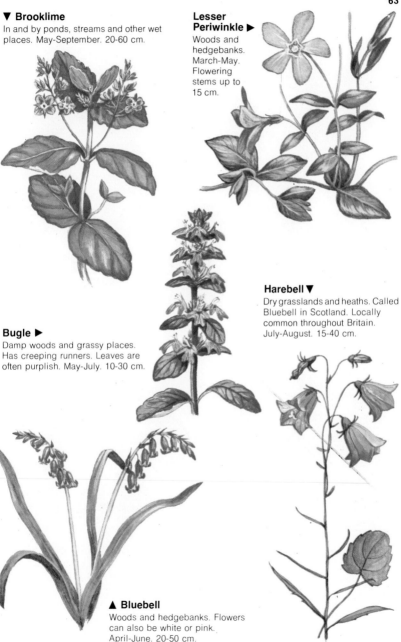

▼ **Brooklime**
In and by ponds, streams and other wet places. May-September. 20-60 cm.

Lesser Periwinkle ▶
Woods and hedgebanks. March-May. Flowering stems up to 15 cm.

Harebell ▼
Dry grasslands and heaths. Called Bluebell in Scotland. Locally common throughout Britain. July-August. 15-40 cm.

Bugle ▶
Damp woods and grassy places. Has creeping runners. Leaves are often purplish. May-July. 10-30 cm.

▲ **Bluebell**
Woods and hedgebanks. Flowers can also be white or pink. April-June. 20-50 cm.

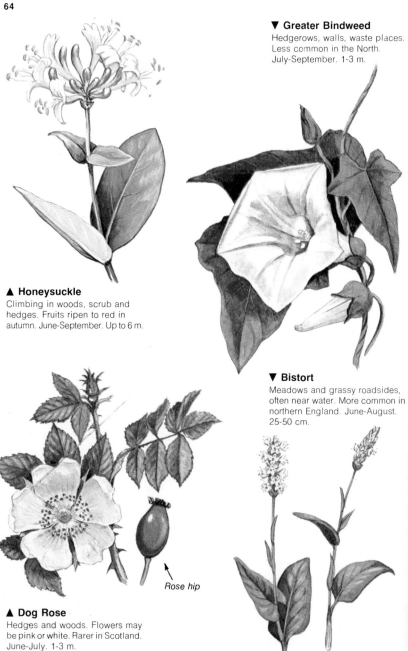

▲ Honeysuckle
Climbing in woods, scrub and hedges. Fruits ripen to red in autumn. June-September. Up to 6 m.

▼ Greater Bindweed
Hedgerows, walls, waste places. Less common in the North. July-September. 1-3 m.

▼ Bistort
Meadows and grassy roadsides, often near water. More common in northern England. June-August. 25-50 cm.

Rose hip

▲ Dog Rose
Hedges and woods. Flowers may be pink or white. Rarer in Scotland. June-July. 1-3 m.

▼ Knotgrass
Waste ground, fields and seashores. A low, far-spreading plant. July-October. Creeping stems 3-200 cm.

Great Willowherb ▶
Ditches, marshes, near streams. Rare in northern Scotland. July-August. 80-150 cm.

◀ Sea Bindweed
Sandy beaches; sometimes shingle. Rare in Scotland. June-August. Trailing stems up to 50 cm.

▼ Sand Spurrey
Sandy or gravelly places. Leaves end in a small bristle. May-September. 5-25 cm.

▲ Sea Milkwort
Grassy saltmarshes. Creeping stems. June-August. 10-30 cm tall.

◀ Thrift
Rocky cliffs near coast; mountains inland. March-October. 5-30 cm.

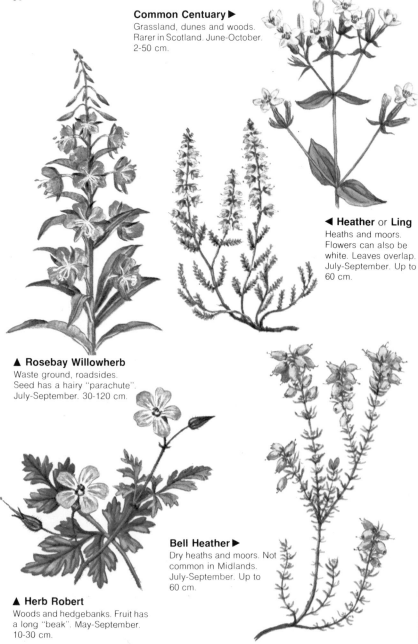

Common Centuary ▶
Grassland, dunes and woods.
Rarer in Scotland. June-October.
2-50 cm.

◀ Heather or Ling
Heaths and moors.
Flowers can also be
white. Leaves overlap.
July-September. Up to
60 cm.

▲ Rosebay Willowherb
Waste ground, roadsides.
Seed has a hairy "parachute".
July-September. 30-120 cm.

Bell Heather ▶
Dry heaths and moors. Not
common in Midlands.
July-September. Up to
60 cm.

▲ Herb Robert
Woods and hedgebanks. Fruit has
a long "beak". May-September.
10-30 cm.

▼ Bilberry
Heaths, moors and woods.
Blue-black berries. Flowers
April-June. Up to 60 cm.

Ragged Robin ▲
Damp meadows,
marshes, woods. Sepals
form a tube. May-June.
30-75 cm.

Lady's Smock ▼
Damp meadows and near streams.
Flower can be pink or white and
lilac. April-June. 15-60 cm.

▲ Lesser Knapweed
Grassland and waysides. Stem is
grooved below flowerhead.
June-September. 15-60 cm.

68

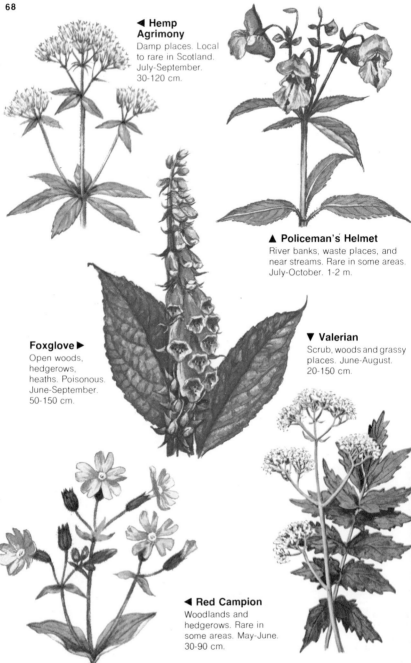

◀ Hemp Agrimony
Damp places. Local
to rare in Scotland.
July-September.
30-120 cm.

▲ Policeman's Helmet
River banks, waste places, and
near streams. Rare in some areas.
July-October. 1-2 m.

Foxglove ▶
Open woods,
hedgerows,
heaths. Poisonous.
June-September.
50-150 cm.

▼ Valerian
Scrub, woods and grassy
places. June-August.
20-150 cm.

◀ Red Campion
Woodlands and
hedgerows. Rare in
some areas. May-June.
30-90 cm.

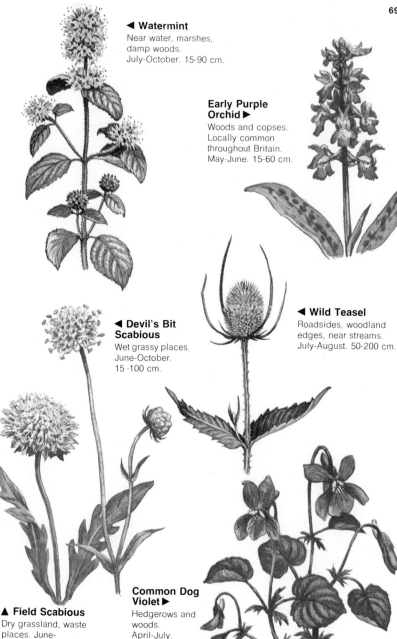

◄ Watermint
Near water, marshes,
damp woods.
July-October. 15-90 cm.

**Early Purple
Orchid ►**
Woods and copses.
Locally common
throughout Britain.
May-June. 15-60 cm.

**◄ Devil's Bit
Scabious**
Wet grassy places.
June-October.
15-100 cm.

◄ Wild Teasel
Roadsides, woodland
edges, near streams.
July-August. 50-200 cm.

▲ Field Scabious
Dry grassland, waste
places. June-
September. 15-80 cm.

**Common Dog
Violet ►**
Hedgerows and
woods.
April-July.
5-20 cm.

Tufted Vetch ▼
Climbs on other plants in hedges
and grassy places. June-August.
Flowers 10 mm long.

▲ Ivy-leaved Toadflax
Old walls, occasionally rocks.
Often forms clumps. May-September.
Flowers 10 mm long.

Sea Lavender ▼
Muddy saltmarshes. Often forms
large mats. Not in northern
Scotland. July-October. 8-30 cm.

▲ Woody Nightshade
Hedges, woods, waste places. Poisonous.
Not common in Scotland. June-September.
Scrambling stems 30-200 cm.

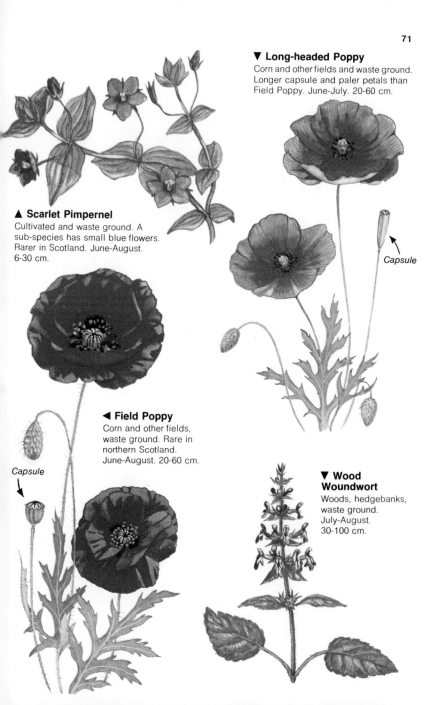

▼ Long-headed Poppy

Corn and other fields and waste ground. Longer capsule and paler petals than Field Poppy. June-July. 20-60 cm.

Capsule

▲ Scarlet Pimpernel

Cultivated and waste ground. A sub-species has small blue flowers. Rarer in Scotland. June-August. 6-30 cm.

◄ Field Poppy

Corn and other fields, waste ground. Rare in northern Scotland. June-August. 20-60 cm.

Capsule

▼ Wood Woundwort

Woods, hedgebanks, waste ground. July-August. 30-100 cm.

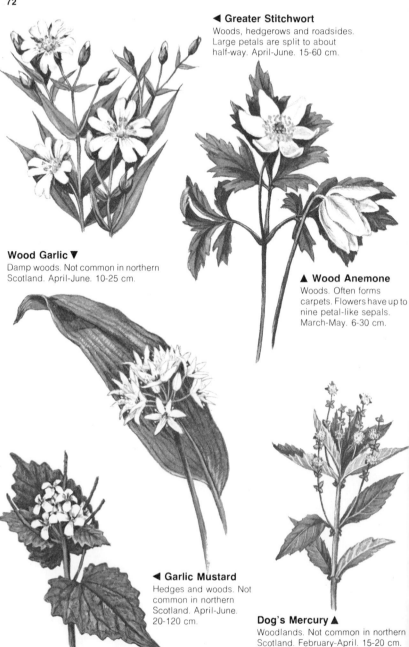

◄ Greater Stitchwort
Woods, hedgerows and roadsides.
Large petals are split to about
half-way. April-June. 15-60 cm.

Wood Garlic ▼
Damp woods. Not common in northern
Scotland. April-June. 10-25 cm.

▲ Wood Anemone
Woods. Often forms
carpets. Flowers have up to
nine petal-like sepals.
March-May. 6-30 cm.

◄ Garlic Mustard
Hedges and woods. Not
common in northern
Scotland. April-June.
20-120 cm.

Dog's Mercury ▲
Woodlands. Not common in northern
Scotland. February-April. 15-20 cm.

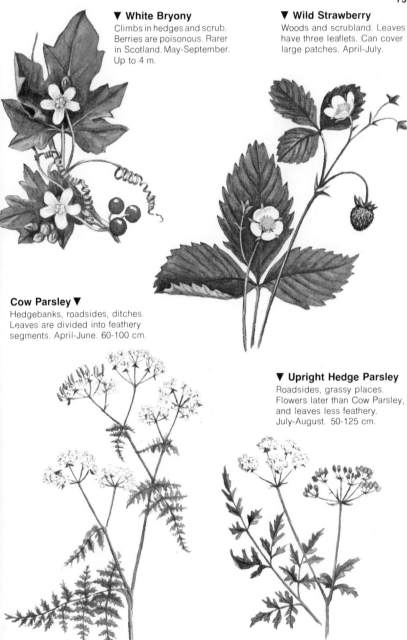

▼ White Bryony
Climbs in hedges and scrub. Berries are poisonous. Rarer in Scotland. May-September. Up to 4 m.

▼ Wild Strawberry
Woods and scrubland. Leaves have three leaflets. Can cover large patches. April-July.

Cow Parsley ▼
Hedgebanks, roadsides, ditches. Leaves are divided into feathery segments. April-June. 60-100 cm.

▼ Upright Hedge Parsley
Roadsides, grassy places. Flowers later than Cow Parsley, and leaves less feathery. July-August. 50-125 cm.

▼ Meadowsweet
Marshes, water meadows and near
ditches. Flowers smell sweet.
May-September 60-120 cm.

▲ Water Crowfoot
Ponds, streams and
ditches. May-June.
Flowers are 10-20 mm
across.

Wild Carrot ▶
Grassy places, especially near
the sea. June-August. 30-100 cm.

Hogweed ▲
Open woods, roadsides,
grassy places.
June-September.
50-200 cm.

Daisy ▲
Short grassland, especially lawns.
March-October. 3-12 cm.

▲ Nettle
Waysides, waste ground, woods. Has stinging hairs. June-August. 30-150 cm.

▼ White Dead Nettle
Roadsides, hedgerows and waste ground. Rare in north Scotland. May-December. 20-60 cm.

▼ White Clover
Garden lawns, grassy places. June-September. Upright stems up to 25 cm.

▲ Shepherd's Purse
Waysides and waste ground. Flowers all year. 3-40 cm.

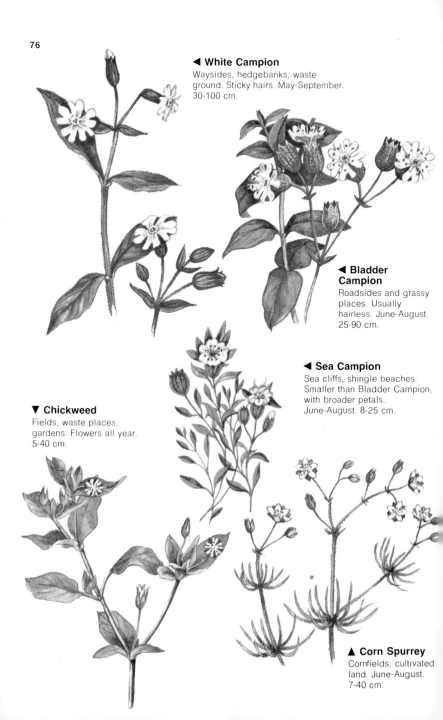

◄ White Campion
Waysides, hedgebanks, waste
ground. Sticky hairs. May-September.
30-100 cm.

**◄ Bladder
Campion**
Roadsides and grassy
places. Usually
hairless. June-August.
25-90 cm.

◄ Sea Campion
Sea cliffs, shingle beaches.
Smaller than Bladder Campion,
with broader petals.
June-August. 8-25 cm.

▼ Chickweed
Fields, waste places,
gardens. Flowers all year.
5-40 cm.

▲ Corn Spurrey
Cornfields, cultivated
land. June-August.
7-40 cm.

Yarrow ▲
Waste ground and
grassy places. June-
August. 8-45 cm.

▲ Ox-eye Daisy
Grassy places and roadsides.
Upper leaves are toothed.
June-August. 20-70 cm.

Sea Sandwort ▶
Sand and shingle
beaches. May-August.
5-25 cm.

▼ Pellitory-of-the-wall
Wall and rock crevices. Not in
northern Scotland. June-October.
30-100 cm.

▲ Wood Sorrel
Woods and hedgebanks. Flowers
close at night and in bad weather.
Petals have lilac veins. April-May. 5-15 cm.

Blackberry

▲ Black Nightshade
Cultivated and waste ground. Rare in
Scotland. July-September. Up to 60 cm.

▲ Bramble
Woods, scrubland, hedges, open
ground. May-September. Arching
stems up to 5 m.

▼ Greater Plantain
Cultivated land, waysides,
lawns. Broad leaves.
May-September. 10-15 cm.

▲ Ribwort Plantain
Grassy and waste places, lawns.
Ribbed leaves. April-August.
Up to 45 cm.

Butterflies

♀

▲ Wall Brown
Woodlands and rough, open ground. Often rests on walls. Not in northern Scotland. Seen March-September. 44-46 mm.

Wall Brown ♂

♂

▲ Grayling
Sandy places, chalk downs. Less common in Wales and East Anglia. Seen July-August. 56-61 mm.

Grayling ♀

♂

Meadow Brown ♀

▲ Meadow Brown
Meadows and other grassy places. Less common in Scotland. Seen June-September. 50-55 mm.

Small Heath ▶
Many areas including open woods, marshes and dry hillsides. Seen April-September. 33-35 mm.

Painted Lady ▶
Dry, open places. Likes thistles. Seen June-October. 62-65 mm.

Painted Lady

Red Admiral ▶
Gardens and woodland edges. Migrant from North Africa. Seen May-October. 66-68 mm.

▲ Small Tortoiseshell
Gardens and open places. Less widespread in Wales and Scotland. Seen April-November. 48-52 mm.

▼

Small Tortoiseshell

▲ Peacock
Gardens. Not present in northern Scotland. Seen August-October. 62-68 mm.

▲ Orange Tip
Woodland edges and hedgerows. Not in parts of Scotland. Seen April-June. 42-48 mm.
▼

♀

♂

Orange Tip

Caterpillar of Small Copper ➤

▲ Common Blue
Prefers downs and rough meadows. Seen April-September. 28-36 mm.

♀

♂

Common Blue

♂

▼ Small Copper
All types of country. Less widespread in Scotland. Seen May-September. 26-30 mm.

♀

♂

♀

♂

▲ Large White
Woods, gardens and open places. Caterpillar eats brassicas. Seen May-August. 62-64 mm.

♂

♀

Large White ♀

♀

Brimstone ♂

▲ Brimstone
Hedges, gardens and woodland paths.
Adult hibernates. Not in Scotland. Seen
June-September. 58-60 mm.

▼ Small White
Gardens and other cultivated places.
Less widespread in Scotland. Seen
May-August. 48-50 mm.

▼ Green-veined White
Open woodland and grassy places,
gardens. Caterpillar eats leaves and
seed-pods of Garlic Mustard. Seen
May-September. 47-50 mm.

Seashore

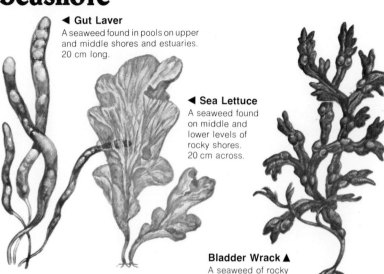

◄ Gut Laver
A seaweed found in pools on upper and middle shores and estuaries. 20 cm long.

◄ Sea Lettuce
A seaweed found on middle and lower levels of rocky shores. 20 cm across.

Bladder Wrack ▲
A seaweed of rocky shores. Up to 60 cm long.

◄ Channelled Wrack
A seaweed found on rocks of the upper shore. 10 cm tall.

▼ Bread-crumb Sponge
On rocks, shells and seaweed holdfasts. 10 cm across.

▲ Haliclona oculata
A sponge found on lower shores in fast currents and estuaries with muddy gravel. Up to 16 cm long.

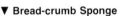

Sea Oak ►
A seaweed found in pools, on stalks of other seaweeds and on rocks. 20 cm tall.

84

▼ Beadlet Anemone
Rock pools at most levels of the shore. 5 cm high.

▼ Snakelocks Anemone
Rocky shores. Not on east or south-east coasts. Can be grey or greenish. 10 cm across.

▲ Daisy Anemone
In rock crevices or mud of shallow pools. 10 cm high.

Dahlia Anemone

▲ Dahlia Anemone
In crevices in rock pools. 15 cm high when open.

◄ Hermit Crab Anemone
On mollusc shells inhabited by Hermit Crab. 10 cm high.

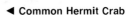

◄ Common Hermit Crab
Mostly lower shore, in rock pools. 5-10 cm long.

▲ Common Limpet
On rocky shores, attached to rocks. 7 cm long.

▲ Common Periwinkle
On rocky and muddy shores. 2.5 cm high.

▲ Netted Dog Whelk
On mud and gravel off shore and on lower shore. 2.5 cm high.

▲ Saddle Oyster
On lower shore, attached to rocks. 6 cm wide.

▲ Common Whelk
Lower shore of rocky or sandy beaches. 8 cm high.

▲ Slipper Limpet
Low water and off shore, often attached to one another. 4-5 cm long.

▲ Common Mussel
Rocky shores, pier piles and estuaries. 1-10 cm long.

▲ Dog Whelk
On rocks and in crevices of lower shore. 3 cm high.

▲ Painted Topshell
On rocks and under stones on lower shore. 2.5 cm high.

▲ Common Oyster
Shallow and deep water. 10-15 cm long.

86

▲ Necklace Shell
Sandy shores. 3 cm high.

▲ Razor Shell
Burrows in mud. 12 cm long.

▲ Common Sand Gaper
Burrows in muddy sand on lower shore.
12 cm wide.

▲ Edible Cockle
In mud and sand of middle shore and below.
4 cm across.

▲ Rayed Trough Shell
Sand or gravel on lower shores. 5 cm long.

▲ Baltic Tellin
In mud and sand of seashores and estuaries.
2 cm long.

▲ Horse Mussel
From lower shore to deep water. 20 cm long.

▲ Flat Periwinkle
Under brown seaweed on rocky shores.
1 cm high.

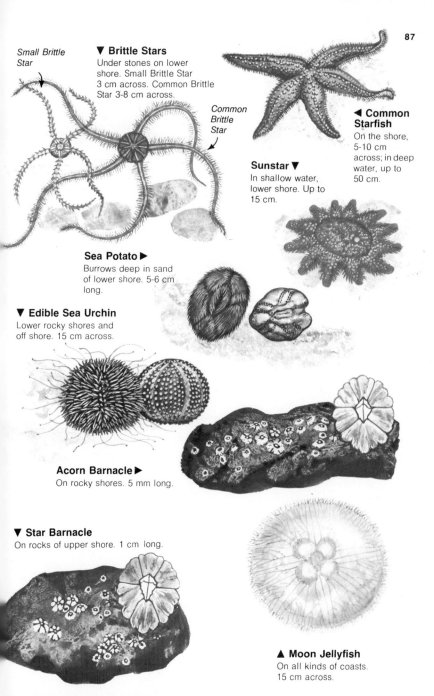

Small Brittle Star

▼ Brittle Stars
Under stones on lower shore. Small Brittle Star 3 cm across. Common Brittle Star 3-8 cm across.

Common Brittle Star

◄ Common Starfish
On the shore, 5-10 cm across; in deep water, up to 50 cm.

Sunstar ▼
In shallow water, lower shore. Up to 15 cm.

Sea Potato ►
Burrows deep in sand of lower shore. 5-6 cm long.

▼ Edible Sea Urchin
Lower rocky shores and off shore. 15 cm across.

Acorn Barnacle ►
On rocky shores. 5 mm long.

▼ Star Barnacle
On rocks of upper shore. 1 cm long.

▲ Moon Jellyfish
On all kinds of coasts. 15 cm across.

88

▲ Common Prawn
Shallow water and rock pools. 5-8 cm long.

▲ White Shrimp
Rock pools on lower shore; shallow waters of estuaries. 5 cm long.

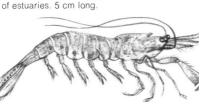

▲ Sand Shrimp
Sand estuaries. 5 cm long.

▲ Shore Crab
Sandy, muddy and rocky shores; estuaries. 8 cm across.

▲ Broad-clawed Porcelain Crab
Under stones on middle and lower shores. 1.2 cm across.

▼ Common Lobster
Only small ones in rock pools of lower shore. Can grow up to 45 cm long elsewhere.

▼ Montagu's Plated Lobster
Under seaweed and stones of lower shore. 4-6 cm long.

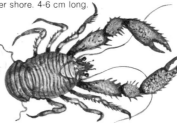

▼ Edible Crab
Only small ones in rock pools in lower shore. Can grow up to 11.5 cm long elsewhere.

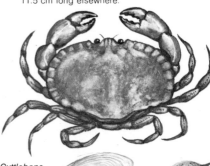

Cuttlebone

▲ Common Cuttlefish
In sheltered bays and washed up dead on strand line. 30 cm long.

Trees

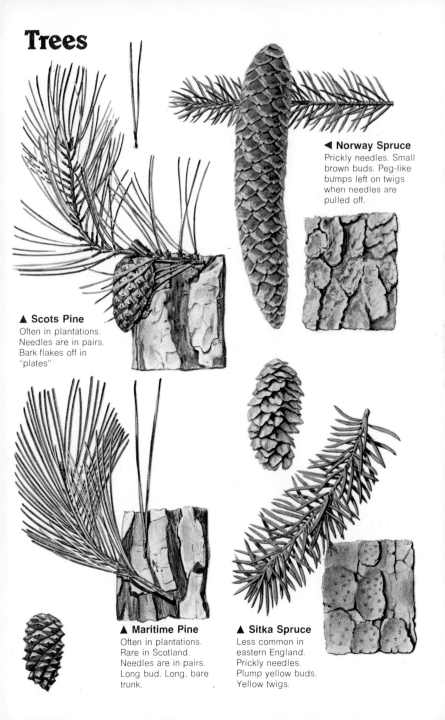

◄ Norway Spruce
Prickly needles. Small brown buds. Peg-like bumps left on twigs when needles are pulled off.

▲ Scots Pine
Often in plantations. Needles are in pairs. Bark flakes off in "plates"

▲ Maritime Pine
Often in plantations. Rare in Scotland. Needles are in pairs. Long bud. Long, bare trunk.

▲ Sitka Spruce
Less common in eastern England. Prickly needles. Plump yellow buds. Yellow twigs.

▼ European Larch
Deciduous. Bunches of soft, light green needles leave small knobs on twigs when they fall.

▲ Douglas Fir
Soft, fragrant needles. Cones have three-pointed bracts on each scale.

▼ European Silver Fir
Rare in east and south-east England. Needles are green above, silvery below.

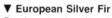

▲ Corsican Pine
Often in plantations. Needles are in pairs. Onion-shaped buds.

Cone

▼ Yew
Often planted in churchyards.
Leaves and berries are poisonous.

▲ Juniper
Needles are in threes
with white band on
upper surface.
Berry-like cones.

▼ English Oak
Less common in
northern Scotland.
Acorns have long
stalks. Leaves are
short-stalked.

Acorn

▲ Chile Pine
Also called Monkey Puzzle. Stiff,
leathery leaves with sharp points.

▼ Common Ash
Less common in northern Scotland. Seeds are in clusters called "keys".

Seeds

Flowers

▼ Rowan
Clusters of flowers appear in May. Berries ripen in August.

Rowan flower

▲ Common Alder
Always found near water. Reddish catkins ripen to cone-like fruits.

Fruit →

Acorn

▲ Sessile Oak
Acorn is usually stalkless. Leaves are long-stalked.

▼ Aspen
Often grows in thickets. Leaves tremble in the wind. White downy catkins appear in May on female trees.

Catkin

▲ Goat Willow
Common on damp waste ground and in scrub woodland. Catkins, known as Pussy Willows, appear in late winter.

▼ White Willow
Common by water. Not in north-west Scotland. Weeping Willow is a variety of this species.

Catkin

Catkin

▲ Silver Birch
Catkins, known as "lamb's tails", are yellow with pollen in April. Bark peels off in ribbons.

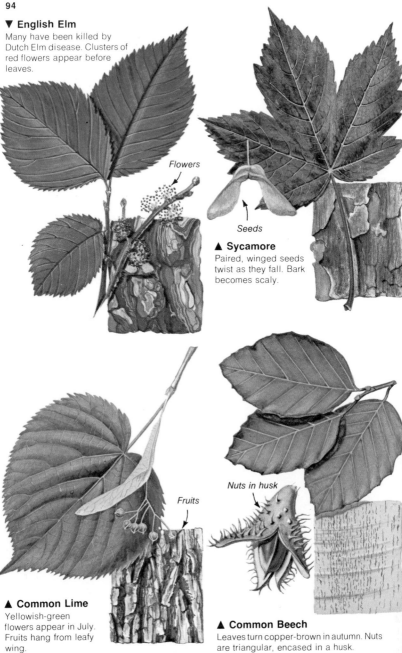

▼ English Elm
Many have been killed by
Dutch Elm disease. Clusters of
red flowers appear before
leaves.

Flowers

Seeds

▲ Sycamore
Paired, winged seeds
twist as they fall. Bark
becomes scaly.

Fruits

Nuts in husk

▲ Common Lime
Yellowish-green
flowers appear in July.
Fruits hang from leafy
wing.

▲ Common Beech
Leaves turn copper-brown in autumn. Nuts
are triangular, encased in a husk.

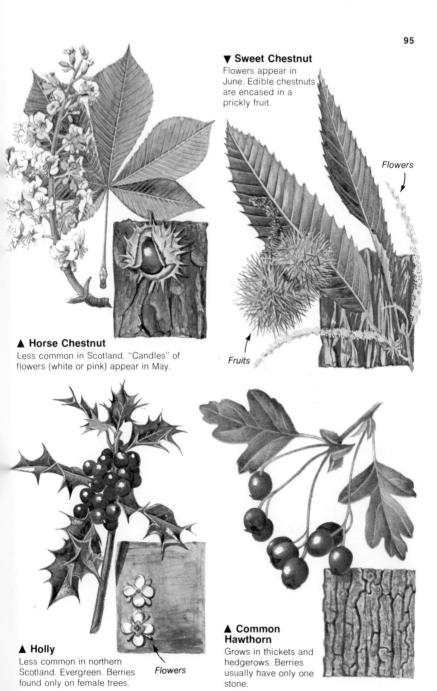

▼ Sweet Chestnut
Flowers appear in June. Edible chestnuts are encased in a prickly fruit.

Flowers

Fruits

▲ Horse Chestnut
Less common in Scotland. "Candles" of flowers (white or pink) appear in May.

▲ Holly
Less common in northern Scotland. Evergreen. Berries found only on female trees.

Flowers

▲ Common Hawthorn
Grows in thickets and hedgerows. Berries usually have only one stone.

The leaves and bark of each of the species shown below are illustrated on page 89–95.

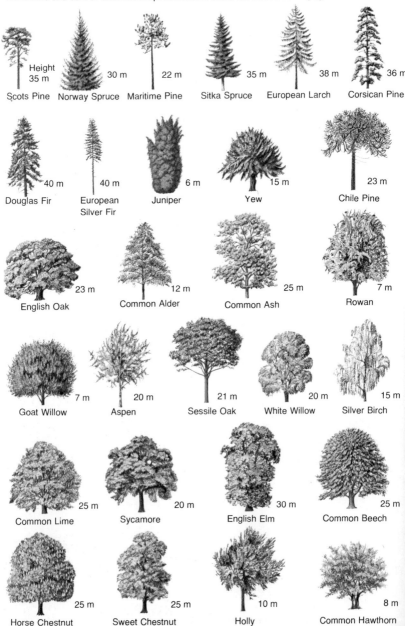

Height
35 m
Scots Pine

30 m
Norway Spruce

22 m
Maritime Pine

35 m
Sitka Spruce

38 m
European Larch

36 m
Corsican Pine

40 m
Douglas Fir

40 m
European
Silver Fir

6 m
Juniper

15 m
Yew

23 m
Chile Pine

23 m
English Oak

12 m
Common Alder

25 m
Common Ash

7 m
Rowan

7 m
Goat Willow

20 m
Aspen

21 m
Sessile Oak

20 m
White Willow

15 m
Silver Birch

25 m
Common Lime

20 m
Sycamore

30 m
English Elm

25 m
Common Beech

25 m
Horse Chestnut

25 m
Sweet Chestnut

10 m
Holly

8 m
Common Hawthorn

Places to Visit

This section describes a large selection of places to visit, ranging from nature reserves, wildfowl refuges and good birdwatching areas to zoos, wildlife parks, country parks, gardens and museums.

The descriptions of the places to visit are grouped under county and listed in alphabetical order. Each place is marked by number on an accompanying county map. Notable long distance footpaths are also marked, but not numbered; their descriptions are found immediately below the maps.

The descriptions outline the main points of interest in each place. They also give details about location, approach by road, and restrictions on opening times. For places outside towns, the Ordnance Survey (1:50 000) map number and grid reference is given, at the very end of each description (eg. OS 142: 205 890). The sheet number follows after "OS" and the grid reference after the colon. With large areas, such as forests and estuaries, a square reference (eg. OS 142: 20 89) is given for the approximate centre of the area. The reference for small gardens sometimes indicates the nearest village.

In the case of nature reserves and wildfowl refuges, the organization which owns or leases them is cited at the beginning of the description. In some, public access is restricted in order to protect the habitat and its wildlife, and a permit must be obtained in advance. This is indicated wherever it applies, together with details of where to apply for permission.

The English Tourist Board publishes a good range of literature on the region, and this is obtainable from the Regional Tourist Office (see page 123). Tourist Information Centres are run in many areas, particularly during the summer months, and these provide both literature and details of current opening times for local places of interest (opening times for some places, such as private gardens, can be irregular and are worth checking in advance). Other useful addresses for organizations such as naturalists' trusts, the Nature Conservancy Council and field centres are also given on page 123.

Cambridgeshire

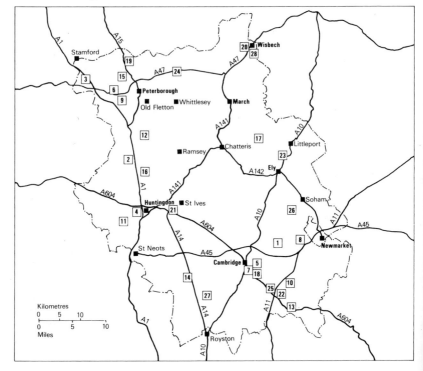

1 Anglesey Abbey
National Trust. Thirteenth-century abbey, later a Tudor house, with outstanding 100-acre/40-ha garden. Picnic area.
☐Open Monday and Friday afternoons, April 1st–October 11th. Near Lode, on B1102, 6 miles/9.5 km north-east of Cambridge. OS 154: 530 624.

2 Aversley Wood
Woodland Trust. Area of Oak and Ash woodland; some well-developed standard trees and a varied flora.
☐Off A1 near Sawtry. OS 142: 16 82.

3 Bedford Purlieus
Woodland. Forestry Commission. Mainly Oak and Ash trees, with many local and rare species in the herbaceous flora.
☐Off A1 south of Stamford, near Wittering. OS 141: 042 995.

4 Brampton Wood
Forestry Commission. Oak and Ash woodland with a variety of other trees and shrubs. Mosses and liverworts in places.
☐Off A141 south-west of Huntingdon, near Brampton. OS 153: 18 70.

5 Cambridge University Botanic Garden
Interesting gardens laid out by Henslow in 1846. Lake, large rock garden and glasshouses. Guided tours available.
☐1 Brookside, Cambridge (Tel: Cambridge 350101). Open all year, Monday–Saturday, and Sunday afternoons in the summer. Glasshouses closed mornings.

6 Castor Hanglands
National Nature Reserve
Nature Conservancy Council. Marsh, heathland and scrub with a wide variety of plants and animals. Leaflets for sale.
☐Permit only (except for Ailsworth Heath):

apply to Nature Conservancy Council, East Midland Regional Office, P.O. Box 6, Godwin House, George Street, Huntingdon (Tel: Huntingdon 56191). Reserve is off A47 west of Peterborough. OS 142: 114 016.

7 Coe Fen

Nature trail. Cambridgeshire and Isle of Ely Naturalists' Trust. Land used for grazing for centuries. Nature trail runs downstream through meadowland beside River Granta to Robinson Crusoe's Island. ☐Some public access all year. Off Fen Causeway, south of Cambridge city centre.

8 Devil's Ditch

Grassland. Cambridgeshire and Isle of Ely Naturalists' Trust. Spectacular linear earthwork about 8 miles/13 km long, dating from between 350 and 700 AD. Crosses fine stretches of chalk grassland. ☐Access by public footpath along crest of Ditch. Ditch is intersected by A45 south-west of Newmarket. OS 154: 568 660–654 584.

9 Ferry Meadows Country Park

Woodland, grassland and lakes. Riding, fishing and boating. Information Centre with natural history displays. Pamphlets. ☐Nene Park, Ham Lane, Orton Waterville, Peterborough (Tel: Peterborough 234443). Open daily, all year. OS 142: 14 98.

10 Fleam Dyke

Grassland. Cambridgeshire and Isle of Ely Naturalists' Trust. Long linear earthwork across chalk grassland, dated between 350 and 700 AD. ☐Access by public footpath along crest of Dyke, which is intersected by A11, 5 miles/8 km east of Cambridge. OS 154: 536 557–571 525.

11 Grafham Water

Birdwatching site, one of the best places in England for watching water birds. Large man-made reservoir; sailing and fishing. ☐Access by public footpath. Off B661, 6½ miles/10 km north of St. Neot's. OS 153: 15 68.

12 Holme Fen National Nature Reserve

Nature Conservancy Council. Fine Birch woodland on about 640 acres/260 ha of fen-peat soils. Rare fenland plants and many fungi. Nature trail and leaflet. ☐Permit only: apply to Nature Conservancy Council, East Midland Regional Office, P.O. Box 6, Godwin House, George Street, Huntingdon (Tel: Huntingdon 56191). Open all year. Reserve is off B660, 6 miles/9 km south of Peterborough. OS 142: 205 890.

13 Linton Zoo

Wide range of exotic animals and birds. ☐Mortimer House, Hadstock Road, Linton (Tel. Cambridge 891308). Open daily, all year. Linton is south-east of Cambridge. OS 154: 56 46.

14 Longstowe Hall Gardens

Woodland walks, lakes, fine trees, daffodils, rose garden and Oxlips. ☐Near Longstowe (Tel: Caxton 203). Open afternoons only, April 19th, May 31st, July 12th, August 2nd and August 30th. Longstowe is off A14, 10 miles/16 km west of Cambridge. OS 153: 30 55

15 Lowlands Farm

About 100 rare species of farm animals. ☐Fenbridge Road, Werrington, Peterborough (Tel: Peterborough 74477). Open daily, June–September. OS 142: 16 03.

16 Monk's Wood
National Nature Reserve

Nature Conservancy Council. Woodland with ponds and clearings. Rich and varied flora. Famed as habitat of rare Black Hairstreak butterfly. Leaflet for sale. ☐Permit only: apply to Nature Conservancy Council, East Midland Region, P.O. Box 6, Godwin House, George Street, Huntingdon (Tel: Huntingdon 56191). Open all year. Reserve is 6½ miles/10 km north of Huntingdon off B1090. OS 142: 20 80.

17 Ouse Washes

Nature reserves. Cambridgeshire and Isle of Ely Naturalists' Trust, RSPB and Wildfowl Trust. Vast area of water meadows between parallel Old and New Bedford

Rivers. Stretches for over 20 miles/32 km, from Earith in Cambridgeshire to Denver in Norfolk. Aquatic and rare grassland plants. Many waders and winter wildfowl. Observatory (Wildfowl Trust at Welney) and public hides (accessible from Welches Dam) open all year. Information Centre. Observatory is accessible to wheelchairs. OS 143: 47 87.

18 Paradise Island
Cambridgeshire and Isle of Ely Naturalists' Trust. Patch of wet meadow and marsh with belts of Alder and Willow scrub, rich in birds and plants. Guidebook, nature trail.
☐Access restricted to nature trail paths. Open all year. South-east of Cambridge city centre.

19 Peakirk Wildfowl Trust
Wildfowl Trust. Reserve with nearly 700 swans, ducks and geese of 100 different species, many very rare. Beautiful water gardens and picnic spots. Wheelchairs and guided tours available.
☐The Waterfowl Gardens, Peakirk, Peterborough (Tel: Peterborough 252271). Open daily, all year; closed December 24th and 25th. Reserve is off B1443, 6 miles/9 km north of Peterborough. OS 142: 169 067.

20 Peckover House
Gardens. National Trust. Fine Victorian garden with unusual trees.
☐North Brink, Wisbech (Tel: Wisbech 3463). Open afternoons only, 1st April–11th October; closed Mondays and Fridays. OS 143: 458 098.

21 Port Holme
Large area of water meadow still managed on traditional lines. Interesting plants.
☐On B1043 and A604, on east side of Huntingdon. OS 153: 235 706.

22 Roman Road
Good for plants and insects. Cambridgeshire and Isle of Ely Naturalists' Trust. About 10 miles/16 km of pre-Roman trackway with verges of great botanical and entomological interest.
☐Access by public footpath. Track begins south-east of Cambridge near Gog Magog Hills, almost paralleling A604 to Horseheath. OS 154: 494 547–636 472.

23 Roswell Pits
Claypits and nature trail. Cambridgeshire and Isle of Ely Naturalists' Trust. Complex and extensive group of meadows and claypits with interesting age graduation. Guides for sale.
☐On A10 near Chettisham, north of Ely. OS 143: 54 83.

24 Thorney Wild Life Park
Large mammals and exotic birds.
☐Thorney, Peterborough (Tel. Thorney 221). Open daily, summer only. Thorney is about 7 miles/11 km north-east of Peterborough on A47. OS 142: 293 036.

25 Wandlebury
Nature trail. Cambridgeshire and Isle of Ely Naturalists' Trust and Cambridgeshire Preservation Society. Hill top crowned by two circular banks with a ditch between them, dating from 300 BC.
☐On A604, 4½ miles/7 km south-east of Cambridge. OS 154: 493 534.

26 Wicken Fen
Nature reserve. National Trust. Fen visited by a wide variety of water birds. Interesting plants and insects.
☐Permit only: apply to the Warden, Wicken Fen, Ely (Tel: Ely 720274). Fen is 8 miles/13 km south of Ely, reached via A10, then A1123. OS 154: 55 70.

27 Wimpole Hall Park
National Trust. Beautiful landscaped park.
☐New Wimpole, near Cambridge (Tel: Arrington 257). Open afternoons only, April 1st–October 11th; closed Mondays and Fridays. New Wimpole is on A603, off A14, 8 miles/13 km south-west of Cambridge. OS 154: 335 510.

28 Wisbech and Fenland Museum
Natural (and fenland) history displays.
☐Museum Square, Wisbech (Tel: Wisbech 3817). Open Tuesday–Saturday, all year.

Essex

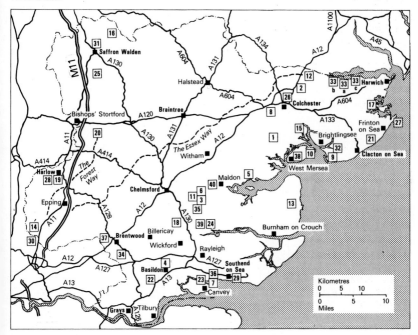

The Essex Way

Long distance footpath from Epping to Dedham via Ongar, Good Easter, Great Waltham, Great Leighs, White Notley, Coggeshall, Fordstreet, Horkesley Heath and Boxted (about 52 miles/83 km in all). Route takes walkers through green lanes, meadows and hills in Constable country.

☐ Guide book available from the East Anglia Tourist Board, 14 Museum Street, Ipswich, Suffolk IP1 1HU.

☐ Route starts on OS 167: 464 014 and ends on OS 168: 060 333.

The Forest Way

Long distance footpath from Epping Forest to Hatfield Forest (about 20 miles/32 km long), running through woodland, grassy hills and rolling farmland. Route goes through Upshire, Rye Hill, Harlow Common, Foster Street, Matching, Hatfield Heath and Woodside Green.

☐ Brochure available from Essex County Council, County Hall, Chelmsford, Essex CM1 1CF. OS 167; 420 995-530 187.

1 Abberton Reservoir

Birdwatching area. Essex Birdwatching and Preservation Society. Largest reservoir in England, famed for its importance to, and variety of, birdlife. Public hide and picnic area.

☐ Restricted access, but an excellent vantage point from the B1026 where it crosses reservoir. 4 miles/6 km south of Colchester. OS 168: 98 18.

2 Ardleigh Reservoir

Birdwatching area. Large reservoir.
2½ miles/4 km north-east of Colchester on A137. OS 168: 03 28.

3 The Backwarden

Nature reserve. Essex Naturalists' Trust and National Trust. Heathland, pools and bogs in disused gravel workings, marshland, and coppiced and scrub woodland. Rich variety of birds, insects and, especially, plants. Nature trail.

☐ Off A414, 4½ miles/7 km east of Chelmsford, near Danbury. OS 167: 782 039.

4 Basildon Zoo
Birds, mammals and big cats.
☐London Road, Vange Basildon (Tel: Basildon 553985). Open daily, all year.

5 Blackwater Estuary
National Nature Reserve
Nature Conservancy Council. Grazing marshes with fresh and saline pools. Salt-marsh and mudflats providing food for a wide range of waders and wildfowl. Varied flora and fauna.
☐No access to private marshes at Tolles-bury. Access off public footpaths on rest of reserve by permit only: apply to Nature Conservancy Council, East Anglia Regional Sub-office, Centurion House, St. John's Street, Colchester (Tel: Colchester 48121). Reserve is near Tollesbury and Maldon. OS 168: 97 07.

6 Blake's Wood
Nature reserve. Essex Naturalists' Trust and National Trust. Woodland with mixed deciduous trees, mainly Hornbeam and Sweet Chestnut coppice. Rich flora and a good selection of insects and breeding birds.
☐4½ miles/7 km east of Chelmsford, near Danbury. OS 167: 775 06.

7 Canvey Point
Nature reserve. Essex Naturalists' Trust. Spit of clay, mud and cockles. Waders and wildfowl. Danger of becoming stranded by incoming tide.
☐On Canvey Island, south-east of Basildon. OS 178: 82 83.

8 Colchester Zoo
Primates, big cats and other animals. Nature trail.
☐Stanway Hall, Maldon Road, Birch, Colchester (Tel: Colchester 330253). Open daily, all year; closed Christmas Day. OS 168: 952 221.

9 Colne Estuary
National Nature Reserve
Essex Naturalists' Trust and Nature Conservancy Council. Saltmarsh, shingle, mudflats and beaches, including the 400-acre/160-ha Colne Point reserve

belonging to the Essex Naturalists' Trust. Large wader and wildfowl population in winter, many passage migrants and some highly localized flora and fauna. Birds include Brent Geese, Curlews, Little Terns and Ringed Plovers.
☐Access to Colne Point area by permit only: apply to Essex Naturalists' Trust Warden, 257 Point Clear Road, St. Osyth, Clacton-on-Sea. Reserve reached via St. Osyth, 4 miles/6 km west of Clacton-on-Sea, off B1027. OS 169: 10 12.

10 Cudmore Grove
Country park. Beach and picnic area.
☐Broman's Lane, East Mersea, Mersea Island. Open daily, all year. OS 168: 064 147.

11 Danbury Park
Country park. Woodland, parkland and gardens. Fishing. For day fishing permits, telephone Danbury 2350.
☐Open daily, all year. Off A414, south-west of Danbury. OS 167: 770 049.

12 Dedham Vale Heavy Horse Centre
Demonstrations by heavy horses and displays of their equipment and trophies.
☐Open Sundays, May–October; daily in August. 6½ miles/10 km north-east of Colchester, near Dedham. Approach roads: A12, then B1029. OS 168: 059 332.

13 Dengie National Nature Reserve
Nature Conservancy Council. Open coastline supporting fairly uncommon species of wildfowl and waders, including Knot, Sanderling and Grey Plover in winter.
☐Access restricted to mudflats. Near Dengie, north of Burnham on Crouch. OS 168: 01 02.

14 Epping Forest
Oak, Beech and Hornbeam woodland with open heath and birch scrub, covering about 6,000 acres/2,400 ha. Deer seen.
☐On A11 to Epping. OS 167: 41 98.

15 Fingringhoe Wick
Nature reserve. Essex Naturalists' Trust reserve on part of Colne Estuary (see above). 125 acres/50 ha of old gravel work-

ings and saltings with two nature trails, an observation tower and numerous hides. Excellent Information Centre.

☐Open Tuesday–Saturday, all year. 4½ miles/7 km south-east of Colchester, near Langenhoe and Fingringhoe. OS 168: 044 195.

16 Hales Wood National Nature Reserve

Nature Conservancy Council. About 20 acres/8 ha of high oak woodland with coppiced understorey, on chalky boulder clay. Oxlips can be found.

☐Permit only: apply to Nature Conservancy Council, East Anglia Regional Sub-office, Centurion House, St. John's Street, Colchester (Tel: Colchester 48121). Reserve is north-east of Saffron Walden, near Ashdon. OS 154: 572 404.

17 Hamford Water
National Nature Reserve

Nature Conservancy Council. Mudflats, saltmarsh and reclaimed marshland. Many thousands of wildfowl and waders on mudflats in winter, especially Brent Geese, Pintails, Curlews and Grey Plovers. Summer birds include Little Terns, Oystercatchers and Ringed Plovers.

☐Access restricted to public footpaths. Reached via sea wall at Little Oakley on B1414 (A136) south-west of Harwich. OS 169: 22 25.

18 Hanningfield Reservoir

Birdwatching area. Good for autumn and spring migrants and winter visitors.

☐Off A130, 5 miles/8 km south of Chelmsford. OS 167: 73 98.

19 Harlow Museum

Folk life, natural history, geology, pond and butterfly garden in the grounds.

☐Third Avenue, Harlow (Tel: Harlow 446611). Open daily, all year.

20 Hatfield Forest Country Park

National Trust. Woodland, parkland and fields. Deer may be seen. Varied birdlife. Lake for boating and fishing.

☐2½ miles/4 km east of Bishop's Stortford off A120. OS 167: 537 199.

21 Holland-on-Sea Marshes

Birdwatching area. Saltmarsh plants and spring and autumn migrants.

☐Off B1032 north-east of Clacton-on-Sea. OS 169: 215 170.

22 Langdon Hills
East and West Country Parks

Farmland and woodland. Horse riding.

☐On B1007 near Basildon. OS 177: 679 862 and 692 858.

23 Leigh National Nature Reserve

Nature Conservancy Council. Mudflats with abundant eel grass, attracting thousands of Brent Geese and Wigeon in autumn. Rich selection of saltmarsh plants. Nature trail. (See also Two Tree Island.)

☐Access restricted to nature trail and footpaths. Between Canvey Island and Leigh-on-Sea. OS 178: 81 85.

24 Marsh Farm

Country park. About 240 acres/96 ha of flat farmland. Boating on river.

☐Off B1012 near South Woodham Ferrers. Open daily, all year. OS 168: 814 961.

25 Mole Hall Wildlife Park

Mammals and birds, including many species of waterfowl.

☐Widdington, Near Saffron Walden (Tel: Saffron Walden 40400). Open daily, all year; closed Christmas Day. OS 167: 549 315.

26 Museum of Natural History

Essex natural history, aquarium.

☐All Saints' Church, High Street, Colchester. Open Monday–Saturday, all year.

27 The Naze

Birdwatching site. Saltmarsh, shingle and mudflats; plants and many migrating and other wildfowl.

☐Off B1034 near Walton-on-the-Naze. OS 169: 26 24.

28 Parndon Wood

Nature reserve. Harlow District Council. Woodland with two nature trails, hides and study centre.

☐Near Great Parndon, off B181 south-west of Harlow. Open daily, April–October. OS 167: 445 066.

29 Prittlewell Priory Museum
Local and natural history exhibits.
☐Southend-on-Sea (Tel: Southend 42878). Open Monday–Saturday and alternate Sunday afternoons, all year. OS 178: 874 874.

30 Queen Elizabeth's Hunting Lodge
Museum. Epping Forest history and natural history exhibits.
☐Ranger's Road, Chingford. Open Wednesday–Sunday afternoons, all year. OS 166: 398 948.

31 Saffron Walden Museum
Geography, archaeology, local history.
☐Museum Street, Saffron Walden (Tel: Saffron Walden 22494). Open Monday–Saturday, and Sunday and Bank Holiday afternoons, all year.

32 St. Osyth Priory
Gardens. Twelfth-century priory.
☐Open daily, May–end September; also Easter. Off B1027 about 4 miles/6 km west of Clacton-on-Sea. OS 169: 121 156.

33 Stour Estuary
Birdwatching area. Wide mudflats and saltmarshes. Good vantage points for birdwatching include:
a) *Bradfield Marshes*
☐Off B1352, 10 miles/16 km east of Colchester. OS 168: 14 31.
b) *Strand at Mistley*
Famed for its population of Mute Swans.
☐On B1352 outside Manningtree. OS 168: 11 32.
c) *Wrabness Marshes*
☐Reached via lane off B1352 near Wrabness, 4½ miles/7 km east of Manningtree. OS 168: 17 32.

34 Thorndon Park
Country park. Lakes, woodland and old parkland. Horse riding, fishing, walking.
☐For day fishing permits, telephone Brentwood 217666. Off A128, 2 miles/3 km south-east of Brentwood. OS 177: 620 916.

35 Thrift Wood
Nature reserve. Essex Naturalists' Trust. Deciduous woodland with pool and clearings. Plants, birds and insects.
☐Access restricted to footpaths and bridleway. Off B1418, 2½ miles/4 km south of Danbury. OS 167: 790 017.

36 Two Tree Island
Nature reserve. Essex Naturalists' Trust and Nature Conservancy Council; part of Leigh National Nature Reserve (see above). Rough grassland and saltings. Interesting mammals, insects and plants as well as thousands of Brent Geese and other wildfowl and waders.
☐Access restricted to footpaths. Between Canvey Island and Leigh-on-Sea. OS 178: 825 855.

37 Weald Park South
Country park. Parkland and woodland where deer may be seen.
☐For day fishing permits, telephone Brentwood 214095. Approach on A12. North-west of Brentwood, near South Weald. OS 177: 571 939.

38 West Mersea Island Museum
Natural history and fishing exhibits.
☐West Mersea, Mersea Island. Open afternoons only, all year; closed Mondays. OS 168: 01 12.

39 Woodham Fen
Nature reserve. Essex Naturalists' Trust and Woodham Ferrers Parish Council. Part saltmarsh, part freshwater marsh. Good selection of waders, marshland birds, plants and insects.
☐Off B1012 near Woodham Ferrers. OS 168: 800 978.

40 Woodham Walter Common
Nature reserve. Essex Naturalists' Trust. Formerly coppice woodland with important bogs in valley floors, currently being reinstated. Rare ferns and aquatic plants.
☐Approach on A414. Near Danbury. OS 167: 790 066.

Lincolnshire

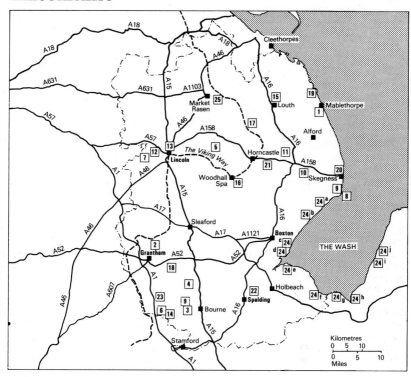

The Viking Way

Long distance footpath running from the Humber to Oakham in Leicestershire. Route starts near the Humber Bridge, goes through the Lincolnshire Wolds, along the River Bain Valley to Horncastle and on to Woodhall Spa. Next, the path goes along the Witham Valley to Lincoln, follows the Lincoln "Cliff" to Woolsthorpe and then follows Ermine Street across Ancaster Heath. Finally, the route passes through the Upper Witham Valley, parallels part of the Grantham Canal, goes past Rutland Water and ends at Oakham. Landscape includes limestone escarpment, farmland and woodland: many sites of interest to naturalists and geologists.
☐Brochure covering first section of route available from The Director of Technical Services, Humberside County Council, Eastgate, Beverley, North Humberside (send a stamped, self-addressed en-velope). Brochures covering remaining six sections of route (five pence each) available from The Secretarial and Legal Services Section, Lincolnshire County Council, County Offices, Lincoln.

1 Animal and Bird Gardens

Mammals, birds and flowers in large gar-dens. Aviary, butterfly display.
☐North End, Mablethorpe (Tel: Mable-thorpe 3346). Open daily, Easter–October.

2 Belton House

Large park with formal gardens, lake, woodland and orangery. Picnic area.
☐Belton, Grantham (Tel: Grantham 66116). Open daily, March 29th–October 5th. OS 130: 929 394.

3 Bourne Wood

Forestry Commission. Ash and Larch woodland with large picnic place.

☐1 mile/2 km west of Bourne on A151. OS 130: 08 21.

4 Callan's Lane Wood

Forestry Commission. Coniferous and deciduous trees, including some very tall Red Cedars, Grand Firs, Oaks. Walks.
☐Off A15 near Kirkby Underwood, 6½ miles/10 km north of Bourne. OS 130: 06 26.

5 Chamber's Wood

Forestry Commission. Woodland noted for its native broadleaved trees; walks.
☐South of Wragby, 11 miles/18 km east of Lincoln off B1202. OS 121: 15 74.

6 Clipsham Yew Tree Avenue

Forestry Commission. Woodland with a magnificent avenue of clipped Yews about 200 years old. Picnic area.
☐Off A1 near Clipsham, 13 miles/20 km south of Grantham. OS 130: 97 16.

7 Doddington Hall Gardens

Walled gardens and nature trail.
☐Doddington, near Lincoln (Tel: Doddington 227). Open Wednesday and Sunday afternoons, May–September. OS 121: 899 701.

8 Gibraltar Point

Nature reserve. Lincolnshire and South Humberside Trust for Nature Conservation. Vast reserve offering a range of coastal habitats rich in flora and fauna. Key migration point: visiting wildfowl and breeding birds can be watched from a hide. Visitors'Centre. Booklet and guide to nature trail for sale.
☐2½ miles/4 km south of Skegness. OS 122: 56 58.

9 Grimsthorpe Estate

Parkland and gardens in the grounds of Grimsthorpe Castle. Fallow and Red Deer.
☐Grimsthorpe, Bourne (Tel: Edenham 205 or 278). Open May 25th, July 27th–August 17th, afternoons only. OS 130: 045 227.

10 Gunby Hall

Formal gardens. National Trust.

☐Burgh-le-Marsh, Spilsby. Open Thursday afternoons only, April–end of September. OS 122: 466 669.

11 Harrington Hall Gardens

Irish Yew hedges, flowering shrubs, roses and lavender in eighteenth-century garden.
☐Harrington, near Spilsby (Tel: Spilsby 52281). Open April–October, Wednesdays and Thursdays. OS 122: 367 718.

12 Hartsholme Country Park

About 88 acres/35 ha of grassland and woodland with a lake. Information centre.
☐Near Skellingthorpe, about 3½ miles/5 km west of Lincoln, off A57. OS 121: 94 69.

13 Lincoln City and County Museum

Natural history section, Roman carvings.
☐Broadgate, Lincoln (Tel: Lincoln 30401). Open daily, all year; closed Sunday mornings. OS 121: 98 72.

14 Morkery Wood

Forestry Commission. Woodland and small disused limestone quarry. Foxes and Badgers may be seen at dusk. Pleasant walks along deer trails. Picnic place.
☐9 miles/14.5 km north-west of Stamford off A1, near Castle Bytham. OS 130: 95 18.

15 Naturalists, Antiquarian and Literary Society Museum

Fossils, butterfly and moth collection.
☐4 Broadbank, Louth (Tel: Louth 3026). Open Saturday, Sunday and Wednesday afternoons all year, and additional days in August.

16 Ostler's Plantation

Forestry Commission. Pine woodland and traces of former heathland. Walks.
☐Off B1191, 1 mile/2 km east of Woodhall Spa. OS 122: 21 62.

17 Red Hill

Nature reserve. Lincolnshire and South Humberside Trust for Nature Conservation. Cliff face with red chalk exposure rich in fossils. Plateau grassland, a fragment of Wold chalk grassland, supports many interesting insects and plants.
☐Free access to quarry and grassland.

Permit only for hillside: apply to Lincoln-shire and South Humberside Trust for Nature Conservation, Manor House, West Street, Alford. Reserve is south-west of Louth, near Goulceby. OS 122: 264 806.

18 Ropsley Rise Wood

Forestry Commission. Some young coni-fers, but also Beech and Oak trees. Picnic site, forest trail. Badgers, Owls, Foxes.
☐Near Ropsley, 4½ miles/7 km east of Grantham. OS 130: 965 350.

19 Saltfleetby-Theddlethorpe Dunes National Nature Reserve

Nature Conservancy Council. Coastal complex of dunes and marshes, sup-porting many birds, insects and verte-brates, including the Natterjack Toad and Short-eared Owl. Grey Seals may be seen in winter, Little Terns in summer. Leaflet.
☐Various access points off A1031 Mablethorpe–Saltfleet. OS 113: 47 91.

20 Skegness Natureland Marine Zoo

Seals, penguins, snakes, flamingoes, fishes, etc. Aquarium, tropical house, avi-ary.
☐North Parade, The Promenade, Skeg-ness (Tel: Skegness 4345). Open daily, all year.

21 Snipe Dales

Nature reserve. Lincolnshire and South Humberside Trust for Nature Conserva-tion. Series of steep-sided valleys cut by streams. Rough grassland on higher slopes and marsh wildlife in valley bot-toms. Many plants and animals.
☐Access restricted to footpaths. Off A1115 Spilsby—Horncastle, near Winceby. OS 122: 320 683.

22 Springfields Gardens

Lake, glasshouses, woodland walks. Picnic areas. Wheelchairs available.
☐Spalding (Tel: Spalding 4843). Open daily, mid April–end of September. OS 131: 265 243.

23 Twyford Forest

Forestry Commission. Mixed conifers and other trees on former airfield. Picnic site

and waymarked walks.
☐On A151 near Colsterworth, 8 miles/13 km south of Grantham. OS 130: 94 23.

24 The Wash

Excellent birdwatching on the mudflats, saltmarshes, farmland and reclaimed pas-tureland close to the shores of the Wash. Vast numbers of waders and wildfowl can be seen, especially in winter, and spring and autumn migrants. Uncommon species often present. Fine displays of flowering saltmarsh plants in the summer.
☐Sea walls provide good vantage points for birdwatching. Access points in Lin-colnshire include:
a) *Friskney*
Sea wall reached on footpaths from Frisk-ney, on A52. OS 122: 50 54.
b) *Wrangle*
Sea wall reached on footpaths from Wrangle, on A52. OS 122: 45 50.
c) *Freiston Delphs*
Near Fishtoft, south-east of Boston. OS 131: 40 42.
d) *Boston Point*
Near Fishtoft, south-east of Boston. OS 131: 39 39.
e) *Holbeach*
Near Holbeach St. Matthew. OS 131: 40 34.
f) *Nene Mouth*
Off A17 near Sutton Bridge. OS 131: 49 26. See also Gibraltar Point.
Access points in Norfolk include:
g) *Terrington*
North-east of Terrington St. Clement, off A17. OS 131: 58 24.
h) *Ouse Mouth*
Reached by public footpaths north of King's Lynn. OS 132: 60 23.
i) *Heacham*
On A149. OS 132: 66 37.
j) *Hunstanton*
On A149. OS 132: 67 40.

See also Snettisham and Holme (Norfolk).

25 Willingham Ponds

Forestry Commission. Mixed woodland, picnic spot, ponds and stream. Walks.
☐On A631, 2 miles/3 km east of Market Rasen. OS 121: 13 88.

Norfolk

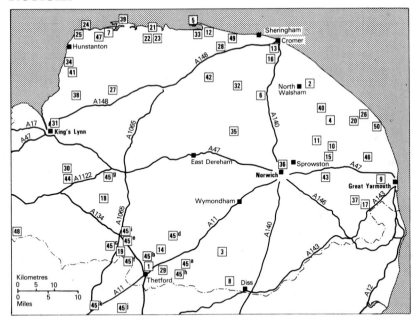

1 Ancient House Museum
Natural history, archaeology and local history exhibits.

☐ White Hart Street, Thetford (Tel: Thetford 2599). Open daily, all year; closed Sunday mornings.

2 Bacton Woods
Forestry Commission. Part of Wensum Forest. Mixed woodland with forest trail and guide. Picnic place ten minutes' drive from beach.

☐ 2½ miles/4 km north-east of North Walsham, off B1150. OS 133: 31 30.

3 Banham Zoo
and Woolly Monkey Sanctuary
Excellent collection of primates and some other unusual animals and birds.

☐ The Grove, Banham, Norwich (Tel: Quidenham 476). Open daily, all year. Banham is on B1113 north-west of Diss. OS 144: 064 883.

4 Barton Broad
Nature reserve. Norfolk Naturalists' Trust.

Beautiful broad surrounded by fens and reed beds. Some rare Broadland birds.

☐ Access restricted to main channels across the broad . Reserve is 11 miles/18 km north-east of Norwich. OS 133: 36 21.

5 Blakeney Point
Nature reserve. National Trust and Norfolk Naturalists' Trust. Shingle spit and sand dunes with saltmarsh plants, wintering Brent Geese and (sometimes) seals. Good migration watch point.

☐ Off A149 near Morston. Access by boat from Blakeney of Morston. No dogs allowed May–July. OS 133: 00 46.

6 Blickling Hall
Gardens. National Trust. Parkland, lake, and orangery.

☐ Aylsham (Tel: Aylsham 3084). Open afternoons only, 1st April–21st May and 1st October–11th October; closed Mondays and Fridays. Open daily, 23rd May–30th September; closed Sunday mornings. OS 133: 18 28.

7 Brancaster Manor

Wildfowl refuge. National Trust. Dunes, marshland and foreshore: habitats for many different birds.

☐4½ miles/6 km north-west of Burnham Market, off A149. Approach road may flood at high spring tides. OS 132: 800 450.

8 Bressingham Gardens

Informal gardens with alpines, heathers, conifers and hardy perennials. Steam train rides past hardy plants nursery.

☐Bressingham Steam Museum, Bressingham, Near Diss (Tel: Bressingham 386). Open afternoons only, Sundays, May–September; Thursdays, end May–September 10th; Wednesdays in August; Easter Sunday, Easter Monday and Bank Holiday Mondays. Approach on A1066. OS 144: 077 808.

9 Breydon Water

Birdwatching site. Tidal waters and mud-flats rich in waders and migratory wildfowl.

☐Access on foot from Great Yarmouth. OS 134: 47 06–57 08.

10 Broadland Conservation Centre

Norfolk Naturalists' Trust. Thatched building floating on pontoons moored between Ranworth and Malthouse Broads. Exhibition on the history and natural history of the Broads. Nature trail. Sales area.

☐Access via nature trail. Centre open April–October; closed Mondays and Saturday mornings. Party bookings in advance from the Warden, Broadland Conservation Centre, Ranworth (Tel: South Walsham 479). Off B1140, 9 miles/15 km north-east of Norwich. OS 134: 359 151.

11 Bure Marshes
National Nature Reserve

Nature Conservancy Council and Norfolk Naturalists' Trust. Extensive fen and woodland with nature trail. Leaflet. Guide for sale from warden.

☐Permit only (except for nature trail at Hoveton Great Broad): apply to Nature Conservancy Council, East Anglia Regional Office, 60 Bracondale, Norwich (Tel: Norwich 20558). Access to nature trail by boat only; boats can be hired at

Horning or Wroxham. Nature trail open May–mid September; closed at weekends. No dogs allowed. Reserve is 7 miles/11 km north-east of Norwich off A1151. OS 133: 32 16.

12 Cley Marshes Bird Sanctuary

Norfolk Naturalists' Trust and National Trust. Freshwater and saltwater marshes. Rare migratory and breeding birds, including Bitterns, Avocets, Spoonbills and Spotted Redshanks.

☐Permit only: apply to the Warden, Watcher's Cottage, Cley (Tel: Cley 380). Open April–October; closed on Mondays. Reserve is 7 miles/11 km west of Sheringham off A149. OS 133: 05 44.

13 Cromer Zoo

Small zoo with a nucleus of circus animals.

☐Howard's Hill, Cromer (Tel: Cromer 512947). Open daily, all year.

14 East Wretham Heath

Nature reserve. Norfolk Naturalists' Trust. Breckland reserve on heath, woodland, meres and grassland. Local plants and insects and varied birdlife. Red Squirrels, deer. Nature trail. Leaflet for sale.

☐Permit only: apply to the Warden, East Wretham Heath, Thetford (Tel: Great Hockham 339). Nature trail open 1st May–30 September, daily; closed on Tuesdays. Reserve is 5 miles/8 km north-east of Thetford on A1075. OS 144: 91 88.

15 Fairhaven Garden Trust

Water gardens and woodland with many rare shrubs. Bird sanctuary and private broad.

☐Warden, 2 The Woodlands, Pilson Green, South Walsham (Tel: South Walsham 449). Open Thursday, Saturday, Sunday and Bank Holiday afternoons, April–September. OS 133: 36 13.

16 Felbrigg Hall

Gardens. National Trust. Lake, woodland.

☐Near Felbrigg, Cromer. Open afternoons only, 1st April–11th October; closed Mondays and Fridays. OS 133: 215 390.

17 Fritton Lake

Country park. Lakeside gardens, woodland and picnic area. Fishing from boats.
☐Open daily, 1st April–first Sunday in October. Off A143 near Great Yarmouth. OS 134: 47 00.

18 Gooderstone Water Gardens

Landscaped garden with pools, bridges, flowers, shrubs, lake and grassy walks.
☐Crow Hall Farm, Gooderstone (about 6½ miles/10 km south-west of Swaffham.) Open Sunday afternoons, June–September. OS 143: 76 02.

19 Grime's Graves

Breckland flora. Department of the Environment. Site of prehistoric flint mines. Breckland flora of heathland and chalk grassland.
☐6 miles/9.5 km north-west of Thetford off A134. OS 144: 81 89.

20 Hickling Broad
National Nature Reserve

Norfolk Naturalists' Trust and Nature Conservancy Council. Oak woodland, open reed beds and sedge beds. A home for passage waders and other interesting birds, such as Bitterns, Gadwalls, Ruffs, Ospreys and Spoonbills. Nature trails, hides and water trail.
☐Access by boat restricted to marked channels only. Access ashore by permit only: apply to the Warden, Warden's Office, Stubb Road, Hickling (Tel: Hickling 276). Open April–October; closed Tuesdays. Water trail operates Tuesdays, Wednesdays and Thursdays, June–mid-September (Tel: Hickling 562 for advance booking). Reserve is off A149 near Hickling Green. OS 134: 420 215.

21 Holkham

Nature reserve. Nature Conservancy Council. Extensive mudflats, sand, salt-marsh and dunes. Corsican Pines supporting a wide range of birdlife. Firm beach and paths allowing access to wheelchairs. Leaflets for sale.
☐Near Wells-next-the-Sea. Access from Holkham Village to Holkham Gap. Western part of reserve accessible on foot from beach at Wells-next-the-Sea and along sea wall from Overy Staithe. OS 132: 90 44.

22 Holkham Gardens

Large garden centre with original seventeenth-century greenhouses.
☐Holkham Park, Wells-next-the-Sea (Tel: Fakenham 710374).Open daily, all year; closed Sunday mornings. OS 312: 88 42.

23 Holkham Hall

Park and gardens. Grounds of eighteenth-century home of "Coke of Norfolk". Large park adjoining, with Fallow Deer, sheep, woodland and farmland.
☐Holkham Park, Wells-next-the-Sea (Tel: Fakenham 710227). Park open daily, all year. Grounds open Spring Bank Holiday Monday; Thursdays, June–September; also Mondays and Wednesdays, July and August. OS 132: 88 42.

24 Holme Bird Observatory

Norfolk Ornithologists' Association. Excellent birdwatching on a wide area of pine-covered sand dunes and marshland.
☐Permit available on the spot. Observatory is 2 miles/3 km east of Holme Village on A149. Access on foot along Thornham sea wall and Holme Beach Road. OS 132: 71 44.

25 Holme Dunes

Nature reserve. Norfolk Naturalists' Trust. Area of salt and freshwater marshes and sand dunes. Birds include Great Skuas, Marsh Harriers, Water Rails, Green Sandpipers, Bearded Tits and many other waders and ducks. Nature trail.
☐Permit only: apply to the Warden, East Wretham Heath, Thetford (Tel: Great Hockham 339). Nature trail open May–September, daily except Tuesdays. Reserve is 5 miles/8 km north-east of Thetford on A1075. OS 144: 91 88.

26 Horsey Mere

Nature reserve. National Trust. Extensive reed beds with swans, winter wildfowl and birds of passage.
☐Permit only off footpaths: apply to National Trust Eastern Regional Office, Blickling, Norwich (Tel: Aylsham 3471).

Reserve is 12 miles/19 km north of Great Yarmouth off B1159. Access by boat only. OS 134: 450 220.

27 Houghton Hall Park
Deer park and stables with heavy horses and Shetland ponies. Informal gardens, peacocks and picnic area.

☐Houghton, Kings's Lynn (Tel: East Rudham 247 or 569). Open Easter–end of September, Thursdays, Sundays and Bank Holidays. Houghton is off A148, about 13 miles/22 km north-east of King's Lynn. OS 132: 790 290.

28 Kelling Park Aviaries
European and tropical birds and some European mammals.

☐Weybourne Road, Holt (Tel: Holt 2235). Open daily, all year. Aviaries are off A148, 10 miles/16 km west of Cromer. OS 133: 08 39.

29 Kilverstone Wildlife Park
Birds and animals from Central and South America, including the Falabella Miniature horse. Deer park, fishing, picnic site.

☐Kilverstone, Near Thetford (Tel: Thetford 5369). Open daily, all year. Dogs not allowed in zoo area. OS 144: 893 841.

30 Lynn Forest
Forestry Commission. Pine trees and old deciduous trees. Deer may be seen. Forest trail and picnic area.

☐6 miles/9.5 km south-east of King's Lynn on A134. OS 132: 677 100.

31 Lynn Museum
Trades, crafts, natural history and archaeology exhibits.

☐Old Market Street, King's Lynn (Tel: King's Lynn 5001). Open daily, all year; closed Sundays and Bank Holidays.

32 Mannington Hall
Gardens. Fine borders, shrubs and roses; also a lake, moat and woodland.

☐Near Saxthorpe (Tel: Saxthorpe 284). Open Thursday and Friday afternoons, May–September. Saxthorpe is 5½ miles/ 9 km north-west of Aylsham on B1354. OS 133: 129 300.

33 Morston Marshes
Nature reserve. National Trust. Wide area of creeks and saltmarshes. Good for plants and birds.

☐On A149, 1¼ miles/2 km west of Blakeney. Access on foot from Stiffkey or Blakeney. OS 133: 010 445.

34 Norfolk Lavender Gardens
100 acres/40 ha of lavender, harvested and distilled in the summer. Products for sale.

☐Caley Mill, Heacham (Tel: Heacham 70384). Open all year, daily, except winter weekends. Heacham is off A149 between Hunstanton and Dersingham. OS 132: 67 37.

35 Norfolk Wildlife Park
Largest collection of British and European animals in the world, all kept in semi-natural enclosures.

☐Great Witchingham, Norwich (Tel: Great Witchingham 274). Open daily, all year. Park is off A1067, north-west of Norwich. OS 133: 11 18.

36 Norwich Castle Museum
Large museum with natural history, social history and local archaeology exhibits.

☐Castle Hill, Norwich (Tel: Norwich 22233). Open all year, daily; closed on Sunday mornings.

Ouse Washes
See entry under Cambridgeshire.

37 Pettitt's Aviary
Rare pheasants, ornamental birds and waterfowl. Feathercraft factory, game larder and taxidermy museum.

☐Camphill, Reedham (Tel: Freethorpe 243). Reedham is off B1140, south-west of Great Yarmouth. Open weekdays and Saturday mornings, all year. OS 134: 42 01.

38 Sandringham Estate
Park comprising 750 acres/300 ha of lakes, woodland and heathland, part of the Royal Estate of H.M. The Queen. Nature trail and museum.

☐Sandringham Estate Office, King's Lynn

(Tel: King's Lynn 2675). Open irregular times, April–September. OS 132: 68 28.

39 Scolt Head Island
Nature reserve. Nature Conservancy Council. Interesting shingle and sand dune formation. Wealth of wildfowl and waders and many notable saltmarsh and sand dune plants. Nature trail and leaflet.
☐No access to ternery in April, May or June. Reserve reached by boat from Brancaster Staithe or via A149. No dogs allowed in April, May or June. OS 132: 82 46.

40 Smallburgh Waterfowl Reserve
Many species of waterfowl in natural conditions.
☐Open Wednesdays, Fridays and Sundays, all year. Dilham, which is off A149, 5 miles/8 km south-east of North Walsham. OS 133: 333 242.

41 Snettisham
Nature reserve. RSPB. Shingle, saltmarsh, flooded pits and vast mudflats on the shores of the Wash. Thousands of winter waders and wildfowl. Scarce plants on the shingle. Hides.
☐Access on foot from Snettisham or Dersingham on A149. Access by wheelchair by arrangement (Tel: Dersingham 40129). OS 132: 648 333.

42 Stody Lodge
Gardens. Formal gardens with lawns, azaleas, rhododendrons, water gardens and arboretum.
☐Stody, near Melton Constable. Stody is off the B1110, south-west of Sheringham. Open some Sundays in May and June. OS 133: 05 35.

43 Strumpshaw Fen
Nature reserve. RSPB. Small broad with reed beds and woodland. Observation hides and display boards with information about breeding and wintering birds.
☐Report to reception hide, Staithe Cottage, Low Road, Strumpshaw, Norwich. Open Wednesdays, Thursdays, Saturdays and Sundays, all year. Reserve is 8 miles/ 13 km east of Norwich. OS 134: 34 06.

44 Talbot Manor
Gardens. Private glasshouse collection of tropical plants. Informal gardens, arboretum and many exotic plants.
☐Open Sunday afternoons in June. Near Fincham, on A1122, 5 miles/8 km north-east of Downham Market. OS 143: 68 06.

45 Thetford Forest
Forestry Commission. Vast forest of about 48,300 acres/19,500 ha on the Norfolk/ Suffolk border. Good places for walks and picnics include:
a) *Bridgham Lane*
Pine and beech woodland with picnic area and two waymarked walks.
☐Near Bridgham, off A1066, 5 miles/8 km east of Thetford. OS 144: 96 85.
b) *Devil's Punchbowl*
Broadleaved and conifer woods around a steep-sided depression. Picnic spot and walks.
☐Turn left off Croxton-East Wretham road north of Thetford, near Croxton. OS 144: 877 892.
c) *Emily's Wood*
Oak and Birch grove with picnic place.
☐2 miles/3 km north of Brandon on A1065. OS 144: 79 89.
d) *Hockham*
Uneven-aged mixed woodland with two forest trails and a picnic place.
☐On A1075 near Great Hockham, between Thetford and Watton. OS 144: 93 91.
e) *Lynford*
Varied broadleaved trees and conifers. Two waymarked walks, forest trail and picnic site.
☐1 mile/1.5 km south-east of Mundford on A134 between Thetford and Downham Market. OS 144: 81 91.
f) *Santon Downham*
Attractive woods with good views, information point, picnic site and forest trail.
☐4¾ miles/7.5 km north-west of Thetford off B1107. OS 144: 816 876.
g) *Swaffham Heath*
Pine woodland with small secluded picnic places and forest walks.
☐On A1122 south-west of Swaffham. OS 144: 79 07.
h) *Thorpe Woodlands*
Campsite on 60 acres/24 ha of quiet

meadowland and woodland on banks of River Thet. Fishing.

☐On by-road to East Harling off A1066, 5 miles/8 km east of Thetford. OS 144: 95 84.

i) *Two Mile Bottom*
Large picnic place among 150-year-old Oak and Beech woods. Two waymarked walks through pine trees.

☐On A134, 3½ miles/5.5 km north-west of Thetford. OS 144: 84 87.

Sites in Suffolk include:

j) *King's Forest*
Spruce, pines, larch and other conifers. Picnic spot under Corsican Pines. Forest trail.

☐6½ miles/10 km north-west of Bury St. Edmunds on B1106. OS 144: 81 73.

k) *Mildenhall*
Scots Pine and Silver Birch woodland within easy reach of the Bedford Cut, 30-foot/9-m Fen drain. Muntjac and Roe Deer may be seen. Picnic place.

☐On A1065 south-west of Thetford. OS 143: 710 745.

46 Thrigby Hall Wildlife Gardens
Asian animals in garden setting; also deer paddock, tropical house, lake and bird house.

☐Filby, near Great Yarmouth (Tel: Flegg-burgh 477). Open daily, all year. 5 miles/8 km north-west of Great Yarmouth. OS 134: 461 125.

47 Titchwell Marsh
Nature reserve. Wide range of waders and winter wildfowl. Reed beds, marshes and sandy shore. Visitor Centre and birdwatching hides.

☐Access via sea walls off A149 near Brancaster. OS 132: 757 437.

The Wash
See entry under Lincolnshire.

48 Welney Wildfowl Refuge
Wildfowl Trust. Hides and large observatory for viewing birds in Ouse Washes (see under Cambridgeshire), including Bewick's Swans and a wide variety of winter wildfowl. Breeding birds in the summer.

☐To book escorted visits on Saturdays and Sundays, contact the Warden at Pintail House, Hundred Foot Bank, Welney, near Wisbech, Cambridgeshire (Tel: Ely 860711). Open daily, all year. Refuge is about 13 miles/21 km south of Wisbech on A1101. OS 143: 550 940.

49 Weybourne
Cliffs. Fossils (Pliocene and Pleistocene) have been found here. Fulmar colonies.
☐3 miles/5 km west of Sheringham on A149. OS 133: 11 43.

50 Winterton Dunes
Nature reserve. Nature Conservancy Council. Large area of sand dunes and acid heath. Coastal animals, including the Natterjack Toad, and acid-tolerant plants. Leaflets for sale.
☐8 miles/13 km north of Great Yarmouth off B1159. OS 134: 49 20.

Suffolk

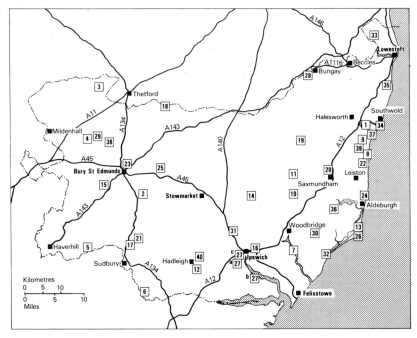

1 Blyth Estuary
Birdwatching area. Hides.

☐ Access along footpaths on southern side of estuary. Approach on A12 to Southwold, then B1387 to Blythburgh. OS 156: 45 75–50 74.

2 Bradfield Woods
Society for the Promotion of Nature Conservation. Coppice woodland. Four types of deer occasionally seen. Great variety of plants due to coppice management and different kinds of soil.

☐ 6½ miles/10 km south-east of Bury St. Edmunds, near Bradfield St. Clare. Approach on A134. OS 155: 930 573.

3 Brandon Park
Landscaped grounds of Brandon House in Thetford Forest. Forest walks, picnic site and nature trail.

☐ Brandon, Near Thetford. Open daily, all year. OS 144: 786 852.

4 Cavenham Heath
Nature reserve. Nature Conservancy Council. Heathland, fens and woodland. Many birds, Roe Deer, Adders and typical heathland plants can be seen. Accessible to wheelchairs.

☐ Free access to part of the reserve all year (except when fire risk is high); permit only for rest of reserve: apply to Nature Conservancy Council, East Anglia Regional Office, 60 Bracondale, Norwich, Norfolk (Tel: Norwich 20558). Reserve is off A1101 near Icklingham 8 miles/13 km north-west of Bury St. Edmunds. OS 155: 75 72.

5 Clare Castle Country Park
Ruins and baileys of Clare Castle with butterfly garden, wildfowl and nature trail in the grounds.

☐ Near Sudbury (Tel: Clare 491). Open daily, all year. OS 155: 774 454.

6 Daw's Hall Wildfowl Farm
Excellent collection of waterfowl and other birds in garden of rare trees and shrubs. Picnicking by permission.

☐Lamarsh, Bures (Tel: Twinstead 213). Open August–October, weekends only. Lamarsh is off B1508 (A133) south of Sudbury. OS 155: 888 366.

7 Deben Estuary
Birdwatching area. Varied eastern shore, with low wooded cliffs and sandy bays. Many types of plants, flowers and birds of saltmarsh and mudflats.
☐South of Woodbridge. Accessible along much of the Estuary. Ramsholt, off B1083, is one access point. OS 169: 30 41.

8 Dunwich Common
National Trust. Sandy beach and gravel cliff and about 214 acres/86ha of heathland.
☐6 miles/10 km north of Leiston off B1125. OS 156: 47 68.

9 Dunwich Forest
Forestry Commission. Pine trees close to the beach. Fallow and Red Deer may be seen. Picnic site.
☐8 miles/13 km north of Leiston off B1125. OS 156: 46 71.

10 Easton Farm Park
Collection of farm animals, including many rare breeds; nature trail.
☐Easton, near Wickham Market (Tel: Wickham Market 746475). Open daily, April–September. OS 156: 276 584.

11 Framlingham Castle
Ruined former seat of the Dukes of Norfolk, set in grassland rich in flora.
☐Framlingham, near Saxmundham (Tel: Framlingham 723330). Open daily, all year. OS 156: 287 637.

12 Hadleigh Railway Track
Abandoned railway track between Hadleigh and Bentley, now a public footpath. Rich chalk grassland with varied flora.
☐Access restricted to footpath. 8 miles/ 13 km south-west of Ipswich. OS 155: 034 419–123 380.

13 Havergate Island
Nature reserve. RSPB. Saltmarsh, shingle and shallow lagoons. The base for Britain's breeding Avocets. Excellent range of breeding birds. Some unusual mammals.
☐Permit only, in advance: apply to the Warden, 30 Mundays Lane, Orford, Woodbridge, Suffolk IP12 2LX. Open April–August, Saturdays, Sundays and Mondays; also half day Thursdays. Island is on B1084, 10 miles/16 km south-east of Wickham Market, near Orford. OS 169: 41 47

14 Helmingham Gardens and Park
Elizabethan moated gardens, ornamental wildfowl and walled garden with rare roses. Deer park with highland cattle.
☐Helmingham (Tel: Helmingham 363) Open Sunday afternoons, April 19th– September 27th. Helmingham is on B1077, 7 miles/11 km north of Ipswich. OS 156: 18 57.

15 Ickworth House
Park and gardens. National Trust. Palladian house with park, woodlands, formal garden and orangery.
☐Horringer (Tel: Horringer 270). Open 1st April–11th October, afternoons only; closed Mondays and Fridays. Horringer is on A143, 4 miles/6 km south-west of Bury St. Edmunds. OS 155: 817 612.

16 Ipswich Museum
Displays on Suffolk geology, natural history, archaeology and ethnography.
☐High Street, Ipswich (Tel: Ipswich 213761). Open Monday–Saturday, all year; closed Bank Holidays.

17 Kentwell Hall
Gardens. Elizabethan manor with lovely gardens, best seen March-May, when spring flowers are out. Many wild flowers.
☐Lord Melford (Tel. Long Melford 207). Open Sundays only, March–Easter; Wednesdays, Thursdays and Sundays, Easter–July 5th; daily except Mondays and Tuesdays, July 20th–September 30th; Sundays only in October. Long Melford is on A134, 4 miles/6 km north of Sudbury. OS 155: 863 479.

18 Knettishall Heath
Country Park. Suffolk County Council. Area

of heather next to Little Ouse River. Western boundary partly formed by Peddars Way. Nature trails.
☐Off A1066, 6½ miles/10 km east of Thetford. OS 144: 95 80.

19 Laxfield and District Museum
Farm tools, archaeology and natural history exhibits displayed in guildhall. Observation beehive.
☐Laxfield, near Halesworth. Open Saturday and Sunday afternoons, Spring Bank Holiday–mid October; also Wednesdays in August. Laxfield is on B117, 8 miles/13 km south-west of Halesworth. OS 156: 29 72.

20 Lonely Farm Leisure Park
Woodland, grassland, caravan park, public house and trout and coarse lakes.
☐Off B1119, 2 miles/3 km north-west of Saxmundham. OS 156: 365 655.

21 Long Melford Railway Track
Abandoned railway track, now a public footpath, running through chalk grassland rich in flora.
☐Access restricted to footpath. Between Long Melford and Lavenham, north of Sudbury. OS 155: 90 49.

22 Minsmere
Nature reserve. RSPB. About 1,500 acres/600 ha of coastal habitats. Many rare birds and fine plants can be seen. Public hides along the beach. Leaflets for sale. Good wheelchair access. Interesting walks around edge of reserve on public footpaths, going through woodland, damp meadows and heathland.
☐Access by permit only, obtainable on arrival or for Bank Holiday weekends in advance from Permits Secretary, Minsmere Nature Reserve, Westleton, Saxmundham. Open Mondays, Wednesdays, Saturdays and Sundays, April 1st–September 15th. No dogs allowed. Reserve is off B1122 to Leiston and B1125 to Westleton (follow RSPB arrows). OS 156: 46 67.

23 Moyse's Hall Museum
Natural history, archaeology and other displays in Norman domestic building.
☐Bury St. Edmunds (Tel: Bury St. Edmunds 63233). Open Monday–Saturday, all year. OS 155: 852 643.

24 North Warren
Nature reserve. RSPB. Heathland, reed beds, woods and arable land. Interesting plants as well as rare breeding and other birds. Nature trail.
☐Access restricted to marked footpaths. On B1122, 2½ miles/4 km south of Leiston. OS 156: 45 59.

25 Norton Bird Gardens
Waterfowl, tropical birds in garden setting.
☐Ixworth Road, Norton (Tel: Pakenham 30957). Open daily, April–October; weekends only, November–March. Gardens are off A1088, 6½ miles/10 km east of Bury St. Edmunds. OS 155: 95 66.

26 Orfordness-Havergate Island
Nature reserve. Nature Conservancy Council. Shingle plants, breeding Terns.
☐Access by boat only. Certain parts of reserve closed from time to time (details on notice boards on site). Reserve is near Orford, on B1084, 11 miles/18 km south-east of Wickham Market. OS 169: 43 48.

27 Orwell Estuary
Birdwatching area. Good vantage points for watching birds include:
a) *Strand*
A137 runs alongside estuary south of Ipswich town centre. OS 169: 16 42.
b) *Pin Mill*
Saltmarshes and woodland.
☐Near Chelmondiston, on B1456. OS 169: 210 380.
c) *Ipswich Docks*
Many ducks and other wildfowl, including the Great Northern Diver, can be seen opposite the main dock in winter. OS 169: 16 44.

28 The Otter Trust
Deer and wildfowl, and four species of otter can be seen. Lakes, riverside walks.
☐Earsham, Bungay (Tel: Bungay 3470). Open daily, March–October. OS 156: 31 86.

29 Rampart Field
Picnic site; interesting Breckland flora.
☐Near Lackford, on A1101, 6½ miles/
10 km north-west of Bury St. Edmunds.
OS 155: 788 716.

30 Rendlesham Forest
Forestry Commission. Pine trees and
heathland where deer may be seen. Picnic
site.
☐3½ miles/5 km east of Woodbridge on
B1084. OS 169: 35 50.

31 The Rosarium
Hundreds of roses growing naturally,
including some rare and unusual varieties.
☐Lime Kiln, Claydon. Open afternoons
only, June–mid-July. Off A45 4 miles/6 km
north of Ipswich. OS 169: 13 49.

32 Shingle Street
Coastal site of special interest to botanists
and physiographers.
☐Off B1083, 8 miles/13 km south-east of
Woodbridge, near Hollesey. OS 169: 36 42.

33 Somerleyton Hall Gardens
Gardens with azaleas, rhododendrons, a
maze and a garden trail.
☐Somerleyton, near Lowestoft (Tel.
Lowestoft 730224). Open Thursdays and
Sundays, Easter Sunday–October 4th;
Tuesdays and Wednesdays in July and
August; also Bank Holidays; afternoons
only. OS 134: 49 97.

34 Southwold Museum
Local history, natural history and
archaeology exhibits.
☐Southwold. Open Whitsun–September,
Tuesday, Wednesday, Friday and Bank
Holiday afternoons.

35 Suffolk Wild Life Country Park
Collection includes big cats, monkeys and
birds.
☐Kessingland, Lowestoft (Tel: Lowestoft
740291). Open daily, April–December.
South of Lowestoft. OS 156: 51 86.

Thetford Forest
See entry under Norfolk.

36 Tunstall Forest
Forestry Commission. Red-barked Scotch
Firs.
☐Access restricted to public footpaths.
On B1078 south of Saxmundham. OS 156:
39 54.

37 Walberswick
Nature reserve. Nature Conservancy
Council. Extensive heathland, reed beds
and mudflats. Large numbers of birds and
some rare insects may be seen. Leaflet for
sale. Accessible to wheelchairs.
☐Permit only off public footpaths: apply
to Nature Conservancy Council, East
Anglia Regional Office, 60 Bracondale,
Norwich, Norfolk (Tel: Norwich 20558).
Reserve is on B1387, 1½ miles/2 km south
of Southwold. OS 156: 49 74.

38 West Stow Country Park
St. Edmondsbury District Council. Grassland, heathland, lake and river and a
reconstructed Anglo-Saxon village.
☐5 miles/8 km north-west of Bury St.
Edmunds, off A1101. OS 155: 81 71.

39 Westleton Heath
Nature reserve. Nature Conservancy
Council. Reserve on wide stretches of
heathland. Varied flora and fauna. Picnic
area.
☐Permit only off public footpaths and
away from picnic area: apply to Nature
Conservancy Council, East Anglia
Regional Office, 60 Bracondale, Norwich,
Norfolk (Tel: Norwich 20558). Reserve is
on B1125 north-east of Saxmundham.
OS 156: 45 69.

40 Wolves Wood
Nature reserve. RSPB. Coppice woodland,
a remnant of Anglo-Saxon forest. Site
retains some links with the ancient forest
ecosystem. Many breeding birds and a
rich variety of plants and other animals can
be seen.
☐Access restricted to nature trails. 2
miles/3 km east of Hadleigh, on A1071.
Open all year. OS 155: 055 440.

Birds to Look Out For

Some species of birds that are characteristic of the different habitats in East Anglia are listed here under habitat. The lists indicate whether they are resident all year, or are summer or winter visitors. Summer visitors may well breed in the region but this is not always the case. The winter visitors may remain all winter or be birds of passage which regularly call in during their autumn or spring migrations.

Summer: April–September
Winter: October–March

The region of East Anglia and Lincolnshire covers a large area and some variation in seasonal visits may occur. For example a few species may only winter in Essex but be present all year in Lincolnshire.

*Regional specialities are indicated with an asterisk. These are species which either have a limited distribution over the rest of Britain, or which breed in East Anglia but in few other regions of Britain.

†Rarities are indicated with a dagger. These are mainly migrants that may occasionally be seen in East Anglia on passage.

Marshes, Fens and Flood Meadows (with small areas of open water)

All year: Bittern*, Heron, Mallard, Teal, Shoveler, Shelduck, Marsh Harrier*, Kestrel, Water Rail*, Moorhen, Lapwing, Redshank, Snipe*, Black-tailed Godwit,*, Black-headed Gull, Bearded Tit*, Willow Tit, Reed Bunting

Summer: Spoonbill†, Ruff*, Greenshank, Little Ringed Plover, Swift, Swallow, House Martin, Yellow Wagtail, Reed Warbler, Savi's Warbler, Sedge Warbler, Whinchat

Winter: Pintail*, Wigeon, Hen Harrier†, Whimbrel, Spotted Redshank†, Jack Snipe†, Short-eared Owl, Redwing, Twite

Open Freshwater (on or near rivers, streams, ponds, lakes, meres, reservoirs etc)

All year: Great Creasted Grebe, Little Grebe, Heron, Mute Swan, Canada Goose, Shelduck, Mallard, Gadwall, Teal, Pintail*, Shoveler, Tufted Duck, Pochard, Moorhen, Coot, Gulls (Black-headed, Lesser Black-backed, Great Black-backed, Common and Herring), Kingfisher, Pied Wagtail

Summer: Little Ringed Plover, Common Sandpiper, Greenshank, Black Tern*, Common Tern, Swift, Swallow, House Martin, Sand Martin

Winter: Cormorant, Bewick's Swan*, Bean Goose†, Pintail*, Goldeneye, Smew*, Wigeon, Scaup, Red-breasted Merganser, Turnstone, Spotted Redshank, Green Sandpiper, Grey Wagtail.

Reed Beds, Carr, Bankside Vegetation

All year: Bittern*, Marsh Harrier*, Snipe*, Water Rail*, Moorhen, Coot, Kingfisher, Bearded Tit*, Willow Tit, Reed Bunting

Summer: Warblers (Grasshopper, Reed, Savi's, Sedge)

Coastal Belt

A variety of habitats come together along the coastal belt. Species seen only on the coast and not elsewhere include:

Summer: Fulmar (nesting on north Norfolk cliffs)

Winter: Snow Bunting (occasionally seen in coastal scrub)

Open Sea

All year: Cormorant, Black-headed Gull, Black-backed Gulls, Herring Gull, Kittiwake

Summer: Little Gull†, Terns (Arctic, Common, Little*, Black*, Sandwich)

Winter: Eider Duck†, Common Scoter†, Velvet Scoter†, Goldeneye, Arctic Skua†, Razorbill, Guillemot

Estuaries and Mudflats

All year: Little Grebe, Cormorant, Heron, Mute Swan, Shelduck, Pintail*, Mallard, Shoveler, Oystercatcher, Ringed Plover, Lapwing, Sanderling, Redshank, Greenshank, Bar-tailed Godwit, Snipe, Gulls (five species as in Open Freshwater), Kingfisher, Carrion Crow

Summer: Spoonbill†, Avocet*, Common Sandpiper, Ruff*, Whimbrel, Black Tern*, Common Tern

Winter: Red-throated Diver†, Great Crested Grebe, Spoonbill†, Whooper Swan†, Bewick's Swan*, Greylag Goose†, Pink-footed Goose†, Brent Goose* Canada Goose, Pintail*, Goldeneye, Smew*, Tufted Duck, Wigeon, Gadwall, Scaup, Pochard, Red-breasted Merganser, Teal, Grey Plover, Turnstone, Dunlin, Knot, Spotted Redshank†, Curlew Sandpiper†, Little Stint†, Curlew, Jack Snipe†, Black-tailed Godwit*, Short-eared Owl, Rock Pipit, Twite†

Sandy Shores, Dunes and Shingle Beaches

All year: Kestrel, Red-legged, Partridge*, Partridge, Oystercatcher, Ringed Plover, Gulls (five species as in Open Freshwater), Stonechat, Goldfinch, Linnet, House Sparrow, Starling

Summer: Terns (five species as in Open Sea), Whinchat, Wheatear

Grassland, Arable Land, Hedgerows, Parks

All year: Kestrel, Red-legged Partridge*, Partridge, Pheasant, Lapwing, Collared Dove, Stock Dove, Woodpigeon, Black-headed Gull, Barn Owl, Little Owl, Tawny Owl, Skylark, Pied Wagtail, Meadow Pipit, Dunnock, Robin, Black-

bird, Mistle Thrush, Song Thrush, Blue Tit, Coal Tit, Great Tit, Wren, Yellowhammer, Corn Bunting, Bullfinch, Chaffinch, Goldfinch, Greenfinch, Linnet, Magpie, House Sparrow, Tree Sparrow, Starling, Rook, Carrion Crow. Jackdaw
Summer: Stone Curlew* Turtle Dove, Cuckoo, Swift, Swallow, Red-backed Shrike*, Blackcap, Chiffchaff, Whitethroat, Willow Warbler, Spotted Flycatcher, Pied Flycatcher, Nightingale*
Winter: Golden Plover, Green Sandpiper†, Snipe*, Common Gull, Waxwing†, Great Grey, Shrike†, Goldcrest, Fieldfare, Redwing, Reed Bunting, Brambling, Hooded Crow†

Heathland and Commons
All year: Kestrel, Pheasant, Skylark, Woodlark, Meadow Pipit, Pied Wagtail, Dunnock, Stonechat, Blackbird, Yellowhammer, Goldfinch, Greenfinch, Linnet, House Sparrow
Summer: Stone Curlew*, Nightjar*, Red-backed Shrike*, Grasshopper Warbler, Willow Warbler, Wheatear, Whinchat, Nightingale*
Winter: Golden Plover, Short-eared Owl, Great Grey Shrike†

Breckland
The Breckland contains heathlands and woodlands (especially coniferous) as well as tempor-

ary meres. In addition to the characteristic birds of heathland, woodland and freshwater, waders (see Estuaries and Mudflats) also occur.

Deciduous Woods
All year: Kestrel, Pheasant, Woodcock, Woodpigeon, Stock Dove, Long-eared Owl, Tawny Owl, Woodpeckers (Great Spotted, Lesser Spotted, Green), Dunnock, Mistle Thrush, Song Thrush, Robin, Blackbird, Tits (Coal, Blue, Great, Long-tailed, Marsh), Nuthatch, Treecreeper, Wren, Bullfinch, Chaffinch, Greenfinch, Hawfinch*, Redpoll, House Sparrow, Tree Sparrow, Starling, Magpie, Jay, Rook, Jackdaw
Summer: Blackcap, Spotted Flycatcher, Pied Flycatcher, Chiffchaff, Garden Warbler, Willow Warbler, Redstart, Nightingale*
Winter: Sparrowhawk, Redwing, Brambling, Siskin, Waxwing†

Conifer Woods
All year: Pheasant, Woodpigeon, Woodcock, Long-eared Owl, Tawny Owl, Great Spotted Woodpecker, Green Woodpecker, Goldcrest, Blackbird, Coal Tit, Tree Creeper, Chaffinch, Redpoll, Crossbill, Jay
Summer: Nightjar*, Chiffchaff
Winter: Sparrowhawk, Brambling

Flowers to Look Out For

Here are some flowering plants to be seen in the various habitats of East Anglia. The species listed include many that are bound to be seen because they are both showy and profuse. Also included are some nationally rare plants that are now restricted to or predominantly found in East Anglia: these are marked with an asterisk*.

Wetlands
The species listed here are those that grow in fens, marshes, damp meadows and on river and waterway banks; also included are plants of acid bogs, marked [A].

Agrimony, Hemp	Fritillary	Pennywort, Marsh	Thistle, Meadow
Angelica	Gipsywort	Pimpernel, Bog [A]	Valerian, Common
Avens, Water	Helleborine, Marsh	Ragged Robin	Marsh
Bedstraws	Iris, Yellow	Ragwort, Fen*	Willowherb, Great
Bistort	Loosestrife, Purple	Marsh	Woundwort, Marsh
Brookweed	Yellow	Rattle, Yellow	Yellowcress, Great
Burnet, Great	Lousewort [A]	Reed	
Butterbur	Mallow, Marsh	Sedge, Fen	*Some Wetland Trees*
Buttercups	Marigold, Bur	Skullcap	*and Shrubs*
Butterwort [A]	Marsh	Sow-thistle, Marsh*	Alder
Chickweed, Water	Meadow-rue, Common	Sow-thistles	Bog Myrtle [A]
Cinquefoil, Marsh [A]	Meadowsweet	Speedwell, Marsh	Buckthorn, Alder
Comfrey	Mint, Water	Pink Water	Common
Cotton Grass [A]	Orchid, Early Marsh	Water	Osiers
Cuckoo Flower	Fen*	Speedwells	Poplar, Black
Dock, Water	Fragrant Marsh	Stitchwort, Bog	Rose, Guelder
Eyebright	Southern Marsh	Marsh	Sallows
Figwort, Water	Parsley, Milk*	Sundew [A]	Willows
Fleabane, Common	Pea, Marsh*	Thistle, Marsh	

Open Water
Deep or shallow. Shallow water may dry out in summer months.

Arrowhead
Bistort, Amphibious
Bladderwort
Bogbean
Brooklime
Bur-reed
Cinquefoil, Marsh

Duckweeds
Forget-me-Not, Water
Frogbit
Marestail
Pondweeds
Pond-sedge, Greater
Reed

Reedmace
Rush, Flowering
Soldier, Water*
Spearwort, Greater
  Lesser
Watercress, Fool's
Water Crowfoot, Common

Water Dropworts
Water-lily, Fringed*
  White
  Yellow
Water-plantain,
  Common
Water Violet

Saltmarshes
Most plants of saltmarsh are restricted to this habitat; those found elsewhere are marked [X].

Arrow grass, Sea
Aster, Sea
Cord-grass
Eel Grass
Glasswort

Manna Grass, Sea
Milkwort, Sea [X]
Plantain, Sea [X]
Purslane, Sea
Scurvy Grass [X]

Seablite, Annual
  Shrubby*
Sea-heath
Sea Lavender

Spurrey, Greater Sea
  Lesser Sea
Thrift [X]
Wormwood, Sea

Sand and Shingle
Species that are confined to coastal sites are marked [C]. The others, though very characteristic of the coast, may also be found in other habitats. Some species are restricted to sand and others to shingle, but many are common to both.

On older sand dunes and shingle ridges, further back from the sea, species of open grassland may be found. Look out too for chalk-loving species where there is an accumulation of lime-rich shell fragments, and for heathland plants where the soil has become leached of nutrients and is acid.

Bedstraw, Lady's
Bindweed, Sea [C]
Buckthorn, Sea [C]
Bugloss, Viper's
Campion, Sea
Clover, Sea [C] *
Dock, Curled
Eyebright
Flax, Purging
Forget-me-Not, Early
Holly, Sea [C]

Herb Robert, Maritime
  [C]
Kale, Sea [C]
Lupin, Sea [C]
Marram Grass [C]
Orchid, Bee
  Early Marsh
  Pyramidal
  Southern Marsh
Pea, Sea [C] *
Plantain, Buckshorn

Plantain, Hoary
Poppy, Yellow Horned
  [C]
Ragwort
Rest-harrow
Rocket, Sea [C]
Sandwort, Sea [C]
Sea-beet [C]
Sea-heath [C]
Sedge, Sand
Silverweed

Sorrel, Sheep's
Speedwell, Wall
Spurges
Stonecrop, Biting
Storksbill
Tamarisk [C]
Thyme
Trefoil, Bird's Foot
Vetch, Spring
  Yellow [C]
Whitlow-grass, Common

Disturbed Ground
These species occur commonly along footpaths and at the edges of fields.

Bindweed, Black
  Field
Bugloss
Campion, White
Charlock
Chickweed
Chicory
Coltsfoot

Cudweeds
Fleabane, Canadian
Goosefoot
Groundsel
Knotgrass
Marigold, Corn
Mayweeds
Melilots

Mustard, Hedge
Nightshade, Black
Pansy, Field
Pennycress, Field
Pimpernel, Scarlet
Plantain, Greater
Poppies
Radish, Wild

Sandworts
Shepherd's Purse
Silverweed
Spurreys
Swinecress
Venus's Looking Glass
Whitlow-grass, Common
Willowherbs

Chalk and Limestone Grassland

Most of the species mentioned here are calcicoles (plants which are restricted to calcareous soils – chalk and limestone). Others are not restricted but are listed here since they occur regularly in chalk and limestone grassland.

Basil, Wild
Bedstraw, Lady's
Bellflower, Clustered
Bugloss, Viper's
Burnet, Salad
Burnet Saxifrage
Calamint, Common
Campion, Bladder
Carrot, Wild
Cowslip
Dropwort
Eyebright
Flax, Purging
Grape Hyacinth *
Houndstongue

Knapweed
Lady's Tresses, Autumn
Marjoram
Meadow-rue
Mignonette
Milk-vetch, Purple
Milkwort
Mint, Corn
Mouse-ear, Field
Mullein, Great
  Hoary
Orchid, Bee
  Common Spotted
  Fragrant
  Pyramidal

Parsnip, Wild
Pasque Flower
Plantain, Hoary
Quaking Grass
Rest-harrow
Rockrose, Common
Scabious
Selfheal
Speedwell, Spiked *
  Speedwells
Squinancywort
Strawberry, Wild
Thistle, Carline
  Dwarf
  Musk

Thyme, Basil
  Wild
Vetch, Horseshoe
  Kidney
Violet, Hairy
Weld
Yarrow
Yellow-wort

Shrubs of Chalky Soils
Buckthorn, Common
Privet
Travellers' Joy
  (a woody climber)
Wayfaring Tree

Heathland

Most of East Anglia's heathlands are dry. Species of the wetter heaths are indicated with [W]. Species restricted to the Breckland are indicated with [B].

Bedstraw, Heath
  Bedstraws
Broom
Butterwort [W]
Catchfly, Sand [B]*
  Spanish [B]*
Foxglove
Gorse
Groundsel, Heath
Harebell
Heath, Cross-leaved [W]

Heather,
  Bell
Lousewort [W]
Milkwort
Orchid, Heath Spotted
Pansy, Wild [B]
Pink, Maiden
Pimpernel, Bog [W]
St John's Wort, Trailing
Sage, Wood
Sedge, Sand

Silverweed
Sorrel, Sheep's
  Wood
Speedwell, Breckland
  [B]*
  Fingered [B]*
  Spring [B]*
  Speedwells
Spurrey, Sand
Stonecrop, Mossy*
Storksbill

Sundew [W]
Thistles
Tormentil
Trefoil, Bird's Foot
Whitlow-grass,
  Common
Willowherb, Rosebay
Violet, Heath Dog
Trees of Heathland
Birches, English
  Oak, Scots Pine

Deciduous Woodland

Spring-flowering plants – marked [S] – are best able to survive in more mature deciduous woods where, although the canopy is complete, there is light shining through in the early part of the year. Summer-flowering plants are often found in profusion in coppice woods and wood pasture in areas where summer sunshine reaches the ground; many characteristic summer flowers are listed.

Aconite, Winter [S]
Alkanet, Green
Anemone, Wood [S]
Angelica
Archangel, Yellow
Avens, Water
Bittercress, Large [S]
Bluebell [S]
Bugle
Burdock
Campion, Red
Celandine, Lesser [S]
Cleavers
Coltsfoot [S]
Cuckoo Flower

Enchanter's
  Nightshade
Figwort
Foxglove
Gromwell, Common
Ground Ivy
Helleborine, Broad-
  leaved
Herb Bennet
Herb Paris [S]
Herb Robert
Honeysuckle
Lily of the Valley [S]
Lords and Ladies [S]
Mercury, Dog's [S]

Moschatel [S]
Orchid, Common
  Spotted
  Early Purple
  Greater Butterfly
  Military*
Oxlip [S]*
Pignut
Pimpernel, Yellow
Primrose [S]
Ramsons [S]
St John's Worts
Sage, Wood
Sanicle
Snowdrop [S]

Sorrel, Wood
Thistle, Marsh
Twayblade, Common
Vervain
Vetch, Bush
  Tufted
Violets [S]
Willowherb, Broad-
  leaved
  Great
  Rosebay
Woodruff
Woundwort, Hedge

Conservation

Britain still offers a variety of habitats rich in wildlife, and areas of wild and beautiful countryside; but these areas are threatened as more land is taken up by industry, housing and agriculture.

When hedgerows are removed and woodlands are cleared, wetlands drained, heaths replaced by forestry plantations, and trees felled indiscriminately, vital habitats are destroyed. The aim of wildlife conservation is to preserve existing habitats and manage them so as to ensure that the species dependent upon these habitats survive.

In Britain the official organization for the conservation of wildlife is the Nature Conservancy Council. They seek to inform farmers, planners and industrialists about environmental problems and to gain their co-operation in caring for the environment. The Council also protects important habitats by setting aside certain areas as nature reserves.

The ultimate responsibility for the survival of our wildlife lies with everyone, if the variety of countryside and wildlife is to remain and be enjoyed by future generations. The Countryside Commission has drawn up guidelines for visitors to the countryside. The main points are listed below.

The Country Code

Guard against all risk of fire.
Fasten all gates.
Keep dogs under proper control.
Keep to the paths across farm land.
Avoid damaging fences, hedges, walls.
Leave no litter.
Safeguard water supplies.
Protect wildlife, wild plants and trees.
Go carefully on country roads.
Respect the life of the countryside.

● *The Conservation of Wild Creatures and Wild Plants Act* makes it illegal to pick certain plants which are so rare as to be endangered, and to uproot *any wild plant* without the landowner's permission.

● *The Bird Protection Act* makes it illegal to take the eggs or disturb any wild bird at its nest.

Nature Conservation in East Anglia

The Fens, had they been left undrained, would now without doubt be one of the finest nature reserves in Europe, providing a haven for countless species of wildlife whose existence is now threatened. The drainage operations of the seventeenth century, which reclaimed thousands of acres of valuable agricultural land, simultaneously robbed wildlife of equally vast undisturbed areas of open water, reed beds and watery thickets.

The ever-increasing demand for fertile land means that more and more of Eastern England's fens and marshes are disappearing under the plough. The other by-products of human populations – pollution and recreation – threaten where drainage has yet to take its toll.

The extensive removal of hedgerows in East Anglia may already have had permanently damaging effects on wildlife, for whom hedgerows are an important refuge.

Even the remote coastal mudflats and saltings are no longer immune to interference from man. Maplin Sands was a popular choice for London's third airport, and is still a favourite site for future developments. The present character of the Wash is further threatened by the proposed installation of a barrage scheme.

Nevertheless, thanks to the foresight of individuals and the co-operative efforts of groups concerned with the countryside, East Anglia has retained some superb examples of its characteristic habitats, many of which are protected and managed as nature reserves.

The Bittern, whose existence is threatened by drainage of its wetland habitat.

Further Reading

Nature in Norfolk: a Heritage in Trust. The Norfolk Naturalists'Trust (Jarrold: 1976)
Birds of Norfolk. M. J. Seago (Jarrold: 1977)
The Birds of Suffolk. W. H. Payn (Ancient House Publishing: 1978)
A Guide to the Birds of Essex. R. Hudson & G. A. Pyman (Essex Birdwatching and Preservation Society: 1968)
Flora of Essex. S. T. Jermyn (Essex Nature Trust: 1975)
* *Flora of Cambridgeshire.* Perring, Sell & Walters (Cambridge University Press: 1964)
The Flora of Lincolnshire. E. J. Gibbons (Lincolnshire Naturalists Union: 1975)
Flora of Norfolk. C. P. Petch & E. L. Swann (Jarrold: 1968)

East Anglia Forests. H. L. Edlin. Forestry Commission Guide (HMSO London: 1972)
The Broads. E. A. Ellis (Collins: 1965)
* *In Breckland Wilds.* W. G. Clark (W. Heffer & Son: 1937)
Hedges. Pollard, Hopper & Moore (Collins: 1974)
The Birds of Britain and Europe. Heinzel, Fitter & Parslow (Collins: 1972)
An Atlas of the Wild Flowers of Britain and Northern Europe. A. Fitter (Collins: 1978)
The Wild Flowers of Britain and Northern Europe. Fitter, Fitter & Blamey (Collins: 1978)

* Book now out of print but may be obtainable from libraries.

Useful Addresses

East Anglia Tourist Office, 14 Museum Street, Ipswich, Suffolk
Field Studies Council, 62 Wilson Street, London EC2
Forestry Commission, East England Conservation Office, Block D, Brooklands Avenue, Cambridge, Cambs.
National Trust (East Anglia Regional Office), Blickling, Norwich, Norfolk
RSPB (Royal Society for the Protection of Birds), The Lodge, Sandy, Beds. East Anglia office: Aldwych House, Bethel Street, Norwich, Norfolk
Society for the Promotion of Nature Conservation, The Green, Nettleham, Lincoln, Lincs.
The Wildfowl Trust, Slimbridge, Gloucester, Glos.

Cambridgeshire
Cambridgeshire and Isle of Ely Trust for Nature Conservation, c/o Botanic Garden, 1 Brookside, Cambridge, Cambs.
Nature Conservancy Council (East Midland Regional Office), PO Box 6, Godwin House, George Street, Huntingdon, Cambs.

Essex
Essex Birdwatching and Preservation

Society, 78 Woodberry Way, Walton, Essex
Essex Naturalists'Trust, c/o Fingrinhoe Wick Nature Reserve, South Green Road, Fingrinhoe, Colchester, Essex. NB: Fingrinhoe Wick Nature Reserve has an Information Centre which is well worth a visit.

Lincolnshire
Lincolnshire and South Humberside Trust for Nature Conservation, Manor House, West Street, Alford, Lincs.

Norfolk
Nature Conservancy Council (East Anglia Regional Office), 60 Bracondale, Norwich, Norfolk
Norfolk Naturalists' Trust, 72 Cathedral Close, Norwich, Norfolk

Suffolk
Flatford Mill Field Centre, East Bergholt, Colchester. Write for details of various courses on natural history which are run at the Field Centre.
Suffolk Trust for Nature Conservation, St Edmund House, Rope Walk, Ipswich, Suffolk. (Holds various public open days on its reserves. Send s.a.e. for details.)

Index

Acknowledgements:
Photographers and Artists

Photographs and paintings are credited by page, left to right, running down the page.

Cover: Dennis Avon & Tony Tilford, John Mason, B. S. Turner, J. Lawton Roberts/ Aquila, John Mason, (painting) Phil Weare/Linden Artists, Michael Richards/RSPB, *Back cover*: John Sibbick/John Martin Artists.

Page 1: Michael W. Richards/RSPB. *Page 3*: E. A. James/NHPA. *Page 4*: R. B. Wilkinson. *Page 5*: (map) Swanston Associates, (photo) D. N. Robinson. *Page 6*: Dennis Avon & Tony Tilford, Heather Angel. *Page 7*: John Mason. *Pages 8–9*: (maps) Swanston Associates. *Page 10*: R. T. Smith, A. T. Moffet/Aquila, John Mason. *Page 11*: J. F. Young, N. R. Foster/Aquila, Dennis Avon & Tony Tilford, Roger Hoskins/NHPA, (painting) Ian Jackson. *Page 12*: J. F. Young, J. Good/NHPA, J. F. Young, John Mason, John Mason, I. C. Rose, M. J. Woods, Geoffrey Kinns, J. Blossom/NHPA. *Page 13*: F. T. Boardman, Michael W. Richards, Heather Angel. *Page 14*: G. Abbott, R. H. Bridson, F. J. Bingley. *Page 15*: John Mason (top four photos), G. Abbott, John Mason, I. C. Rose, R. B. Wilkinson. *Page 16*: C. F. Durell, D. Fisher. *Page 17*: E. Soothill/Aquila, F. Greenaway/NHPA, R. H. Bridson, J. F. Young, J. F. Young, R. Mearns. *Page 18*: M. Wright, G. Abbott, R. T. Smith, J. Good/NHPA, D. Cheyne, G. Abbott. *Page 19*: John Mason, John Mason, G. Abbott, C. F. Durell, J. F. Young, John Mason. *Page 20*: B. Hawkes/NHPA, R. E. Scott, R. B. Wilkinson. *Page 21*: Michael W. Richards/RSPB, J. F. Young, I. C. Rose, C. J. Legg, R. B. Wilkinson, John Mason. *Page 22*: John Mason, R. H. Bridson, Ros Evans, John Mason, C. F. Durell, Ros Evans, G. Abbott, G. Abbott. *Page 23*: John Mason, John Mason, R. H. Bridson. *Page 24*: F. T. Boardman, I. C. Rose, I. C. Rose. *Page 25*: R. B. Wilkinson, Dennis Avon & Tony Tilford, C. S. Waller, F. J. Bingley, F. J. Bingley, John Mason. *Page 26*: Dennis Avon & Tony Tilford, D. N. Dalton/NHPA, F. J. Bingley, G. Abbott. *Page 27*: F. J. Bingley. *Page 28*: I. C. Rose, John Mason, John Mason, I. C. Rose, John Mason, John Mason, (painting) John Sibbick/John Martin Artists. *Page 29*: John Mason. *Page 30*: John Mason, B. Kinloch, Dennis Avon & Tony Tilford, Ros Evans, Ros Evans, D. Cheyne, John Mason, John Mason, M. K. Lofthouse. *Page 31*: Heather Angel, R. T. Smith, F. T. Boardman, Heather Angel. *Page 32*: R. T. Smith, R. Powley/Aquila, Dennis Avon & Tony Tilford. *Page 33*: John Sibbick/John Martin Artists. *Pages 34–53*: Trevor Boyer. *Page 54*: Chris Shields/Wilcock Riley. *Page 55*: David Wright/Tudor Art, Chris Shields/Wilcock Riley. *Page 56*: Chris Shields/Wilcock Riley. *Pages 57–70*: Hilary Burn. *Page 71*: Hilary Burn, Michelle Emblem/Middletons, Hilary Burn. *Pages 72–8*: Hilary Burn. *Pages 79–80*: Joyce Bee. *Page 81*: Joyce Bee, Chris Shields/Wilcock Riley. *Page 82*: Joyce Bee. *Pages 83–5*: John Barber. *Page 86*: John Barber, Michelle Emblem/Middletons. *Pages 87–8*: John Barber. *Pages 89–95*: Annabel Milne & Peter Stebbing. *Page 96*: Annabel Milne & Peter Stebbing, Bob Bampton/Garden Studio (Hawthorn). *Page 97*: NHPA. Maps on pages 98, 101, 105, 108, 114: Swanston Associates. *Page 122*: John Sibbick/John Martin Artists.